D0808548

Intro To
ARMY LIFE ★

A HANDBOOK FOR SPOUSES AND SIGNIFICANT OTHERS ENTERING THE ARMY LIFESTYLE

ALLISON MEWES

Intro To Army Life: A Handbook for Spouses and Significant Others
Entering the Army Lifestyle
by Allison Mewes

ISBN: 978-1-61206-026-2

To book the author to speak, do a book signing in your area, or buy books in large quantities, please email Allison Mewes at allison@introtoarmylife.com

Published by

ALOHA
AlohaPublishing.com

First Printing

Printed in the United States of America

TO MY HUSBAND, RUSTY MEWES

THE ARMY SPOUSE PRAYER

Dear Lord,

Give me the greatness of heart to see the difference between duty and my soldier's love for me. Give me understanding that I may know, when duty calls they must go. Give me a task to do each day, to fill the time when he's away. And Lord, when he's in a foreign land, keep him safe in your loving hand. When duty is in the field, please protect him and be his shield. When deployment is so long, please stay with me and keep me strong. Amen.

— Anonymous

CONTENTS

FOREWORD

I've been a military spouse for over 12 years now. I'm so proud of my husband and his choice to live a life of service to our country, and I'm thrilled that I get to be by his side (most of the time). Being around service members and Army spouses is probably one of the greatest benefits my husband and I have found in our Army life. I get emotional during the national anthem, I love Army ceremonies and traditions, and I even know the Army song by heart.

While I love my Army lifestyle, I will tell you the truth: it can be overwhelming. You will have to make tough decisions on your own at times. You might go weeks without speaking to your soldier while he or she is deployed. You will wonder and worry and feel as if no one can possibly understand what you're going through, and your civilian friends will sometimes seem out of reach.

Despite these difficulties, I really have seen a change in the way spouses are treated and respected. The life of an Army spouse is one of triumph, traveling and cultural expansion, finding new friends in the most unexpected places and always being ready for an adventure. No one hears or reads about the lives we impact as Army spouses because we're not glory hounds—we do things because they're the right things to do, because they're good for the community.

Always keep in mind that there are things out there you can do with your life, like volunteer, go to college or start a career. You don't just have to be dependent on your soldier. You've got to have a dream. If you don't, you're not working towards anything, and that can make Army life more difficult. It can even be a small dream, but you've got to have a dream.

It's a roller coaster ride, but in the end, it's worth it. I love being an Army spouse. So to all of you amazing, smart and capable military spouses out there, I commend you and your service, and I am truly honored to be serving with you.

All the Way, Airborne. HOOAH!

Crystal Cavalier
2011 Army Spouse of the Year

INTRODUCTION

Congratulations! If you are reading this book, you must be the proud spouse or significant other of an Army soldier. If you weren't raised in the Army, the culture may be an entirely new experience for you. In fact, it might even seem like a different world. Since only 1 percent of the population serves in the U.S. military at any given time, you can be very proud of your soldier's commitment to serving our country.

First things first: if you're not in the military, you are considered a "civilian"; if you're married to a soldier, you are a military dependent. You may have already figured out that the military lifestyle is a little different than the civilian lifestyle—and if not, you will soon. There are unwritten rules you're expected to follow, as well as protocols and acronyms you'll need to know to be able to adjust to the military lifestyle. You most likely won't learn about the unspoken etiquette or perks available to military families unless someone tells you or you do the legwork. But, there is good news: there are a lot of other men and women in the same place as you are right now, and there is a wealth of information available to help you navigate through your new Army life.

Intro to Army Life provides the basics of what you need to know and should expect when you love an Army soldier. It is not created to be a comprehensive guide to each subject—there is so much information out there that each chapter could be its own book! It will, however, provide you with information and resources for the topic most relevant to you and make the transition a little easier and more fun. This book serves as both an introduction to Army life and a go-to guide when you encounter new things in your military experience, and the chapters are carefully grouped and named to be an easy reference when you need information about a particular subject. It is everything I wanted to know when I became a proud Army girlfriend and, later, wife. I learned the hard way on a few things, so I'm here to ensure that you don't make the same mistakes!

Since upwards of 10 percent of service members are women, this handbook is written for both male and female spouses and significant others. You'll notice that I typically refer to military personnel as "your soldier," rather than he or she, as often as possible.

Note: As with all things military, information in this book is subject to change and may vary slightly, depending on if your soldier is Active Duty, Reserve or National Guard. When in doubt, please refer to the references provided throughout; you will see a "Resource" section at the end of most chapters. You can also ask questions on the *Intro to Army Life* Facebook page www.facebook.com/IntroToArmyLife.

WELCOME TO ARMY LIFE

MY INTRO TO ARMY LIFE

Most people don't choose to be a military wife or husband, and I am one of those people. You see, I waited a long time to find the man of my dreams, and he just so happened to be an Active Duty Army National Guardsman. Like many couples, we were set up on a blind date by a mutual friend (thank you, Jen!). Before the date, he told Jen he wasn't looking for anything serious, as he would be leaving for a yearlong deployment within the next couple months. Alas, true love won out, and after only six months, we were engaged. We married just one and a half months later—talk about a whirlwind romance!

Just as the romance was a whirlwind, so was the introduction to Army life. After just one week of wedded bliss, my soldier was ordered to AT (Annual Training). AT lasted three long weeks in which we couldn't speak to or see one another. After AT, he was home for five days and then deployed to the Middle East for a year. Thus began my Army lifestyle. In the first year we were married, we were together a total of about 24 days.

Now, I'll be honest: I didn't know *anything* about the military when I first met my husband. I didn't grow up in a military family or near a military base, and I certainly didn't know any soldiers who could prepare me for what it would be like. While my husband and I were dating, I struggled to understand what he was talking about when he used military lingo and acronyms, why he acted how he did at certain times and what he actually did for a living. Thankfully, he was patient with me during my question-asking sessions. After he deployed, however, I was on my own, without my patient husband to explain things. I was alone, trying to figure out insurance benefits (TRICARE), family matters and simply how to cope for an entire year without my new husband.

This frequently happens to military spouses and significant others—when their soldiers deploy, they are left in a complicated, super-structured culture they don't fully understand. It is easy to withdraw and become isolated during these times, and a lot of military spouses feel misunderstood or alone. It is heartbreaking to see depressed and struggling spouses during a deployment. Most of them haven't heard about the FRG (Family Readiness Group) and don't know about the many resources available to them. A lot of spouses try to do everything on their own, and this creates a lot of unnecessary anxiety.

But there is hope. This handbook provides the foundation of knowledge you need to become familiarized with the many resources available to you as a military spouse or significant other. There is no support quite like the support of a fellow Army spouse or significant other—we're all in this together! HOOAH!

ATTRIBUTES TO LIVE BY

It's been said that being a military spouse is the toughest job in the military. This may be true at times, and it is definitely not an easy life. The military has a saying: if the military wanted a soldier to have a spouse, they would have issued them one! While this might be an exaggeration, it gives you an idea of the regimented lifestyle that Army spouses (often unknowingly) sign up for when they say, "I do." It isn't a life for the faint of heart.

That being said, it is important to remember that the military lifestyle is what YOU make of it. With this in mind, there are a few personal attributes that will help you as you begin your military journey. Keep these attributes, along with a sprinkling of good old-fashioned faith, in your back pocket—you will need them often:

- Positivity
- Optimism
- Flexibility
- Patience
- Resilience

Developing these personal attributes will take practice, but they will make the experience a much more pleasant one. By staying positive, optimistic and flexible, practicing patience in frustrating circumstances and remaining resilient in even the most difficult times, you support your hero. You demonstrate commitment to your service member and your marriage, and you show pride for your soldier and family.

The need for these attributes is especially clear when you look at the statistics. As a military spouse, the odds are against you. According to the DoD (Department of Defense), the military divorce rate was at 3.6 percent in 2010, which is higher than the civilian rate of 3.4 percent.[1] In the military, spouses may experience extended absences from one another, raise kids alone and only be able to communicate for short, scheduled lengths of time. It can be tough.

But love is a choice, not a feeling. You have to choose to love when times get tough. Communicate openly with your soldier to find what works best for the two of you to remain connected when you're apart.

In the July 2011 issue of *Military Spouse Magazine*, First Lady Michelle Obama said, "When you meet the average military spouse, she is a pretty phenomenal woman in so many ways. There are not many women who could handle multiple deployments, manage frequent changes, deal with children and keeping them calm and stable [and] hold down a job in this economy." It's true. Consider yourself an extraordinary person and lucky to have such a brave soldier at work, defending the freedom of our country.

The truth is that you will need to learn to suck it up a lot of the time. You're going to have to attend mandatory barbecues, and special events (which usually aren't the best planned or most entertaining events you've

---

[1] "Living the Army Values." U.S. Army. http://www.goArmy.com/soldier-life/being-a-soldier/living-the-Army-values.html.

ever attended). I have been to a handful of these military events in which I've asked my soldier, "How long do we have to stay?" Regardless of the circumstance, put a smile on your face, be kind, engage with others and make the best of it. Continually review the five personal attributes, and try to apply them in all situations. And always remember: military life is what you make of it.

> *"God bless the flexible of heart,*
> *because they don't break when bent."*
> — *Unknown*

Army Family Team Building (AFTB) has training modules for you to learn everything you want and need to know about the Army. Visit the Army Reserve Family Programs website at http://www.arfp.org.

5 THINGS TO LEARN, UNDERSTAND AND ACCEPT

Because the U.S. Army has been an institution since 1775, it has rules and regulations that have been around much longer than you have. Your soldier has to abide by these rules and, therefore, so do you—especially if you live on post. Keep in mind that the Army isn't going to adjust to your lifestyle; it's the other way around. It can be difficult, but you're an Army spouse or significant other, and you're a tough cookie!

We've already talked about necessary personal attributes, familiarizing yourself with the base and showing interest in your soldier's life and career. Now, let's take a look at a few things you need to learn, understand and accept when entering the Army lifestyle.

1. **Be flexible.** The military doesn't care about holidays, plans or vacations. Regardless of whether you have grand plans for a family reunion or a trip you've been anticipating for a year, deployment or a drill weekend trumps your trip. Always be ready to change your plans or go solo. Military families get used to spending special occasions without their soldiers, and you will, too. I know this all too well: since my husband was gone our entire first year of marriage, I don't think people believed I was actually married!

2. **Accept the unknown.** The unknown is normal in the military lifestyle, especially surrounding deployments. While there may be a target departure date, sometimes soldiers don't know when they are leaving until the day before they are expected to hop on the plane. You may not know when your spouse is coming home on leave from a deployment until you get a call after they land on U.S. soil, saying he will be home in five hours. And remember: even if there is a plan, it is always subject to change at the military's discretion.

3. **Always be prepared.** Your loved one could be called upon to mobilize for a deployment at any time. Are you entered into DEERS (Defense Enrollment Eligibility Reporting System)? Do you both have your wills drafted? Do you have a support system to help when your soldier is away? Do you know who to call if your refrigerator or garage door breaks? These are things you need to plan for ahead of time; while your soldier is gone, things can, and most often do, go wrong. Two spouses in my FRG (Family Readiness Group) had their sewers back up and flood their bathrooms and basements while their soldiers were deployed.

4. **Know your soldier's social security number.** Get to know your loved one's social security number…and fast. Your spouse is considered your "sponsor," and his social security number is how you are recognized in the military system.

5. **Be curious and persistent.** There are countless resources available to military families. But here's a secret: no one will tell you about them, and you will have to seek them out yourself. Ask about these resources. If no one responds, keep asking until they do respond or direct you to someone who can help. Remember the important personal attribute of persistence? You'll use it often!

Hurry up and wait. You will find yourself doing this a lot in the military. Oftentimes, you'll need to prepare quickly for an activity that is then delayed.

RESOURCE

If you are a spouse and want to learn more about the Army, you can sign up for an AKO (Army Knowledge Online) account. AKO is an Army portal for soldiers and Department of the Army (DA) civilians, which provides access to installation and travel information, training links, career opportunities (military and civilian) and the latest Army news; visit www.us.army.mil. To register for an account and access the site, you must first be entered into the DEERS system (see page 85).

UNDERSTANDING YOUR SOLDIER

UNDERSTANDING ARMY LIFE

The first step to understanding Army life is adopting a willingness to ask your soldier questions. Showing interest in your soldier's life makes him or her feel like you care. It also opens up conversations and stories about military experiences, and you'll feel more engaged and included in your soldier's career.

Since the majority of civilians don't typically frequent an Army post (also known as an installation or base), what goes on inside the security checkpoint is often a mystery—especially if your soldier is in the National Guard or Reserve and your family doesn't live on or even near a post. But even if a military base is new to you, there are a few ways that you can get to know your way around a base and ease into the military lifestyle. If possible, you should elicit the help of your loved one to make this process easier. If you are married and live on base, you will get a crash course, with your soldier by your side, introducing you to the ins and outs of military life. But if you move to a base shortly before your soldier deploys, you may need to tackle a few of these on your own.

The following tips are most applicable if you're a significant other living off post and aren't yet ingrained in the daily military lifestyle. With the assistance of your loved one, if possible, these will help you adjust to your new life on or off post.

+ Take a driving tour of the base.

+ Locate the post exchange (PX) and commissary.

- Meet the other soldiers in his unit so you can place faces with names.

- Meet spouses and significant others of soldiers.
  Trust me, they will be a huge source of support for you—especially during a deployment.

- Ask your soldier to show you his workspace and office, if applicable.

- Have your soldier explain his uniform to you, as well as what each of the various medals, ribbons and patches stand for (see page 61 for a guide to understanding uniforms).

- View pictures from Basic Training and/or previous duty stations.

- Get involved in spouse support groups.

- Get involved in post activities.

If you have to navigate a new installation on your own, be sure to ask the other military spouses how to get involved on your post. If the spouse you ask doesn't know, ask another one…and keep asking until you find someone to help you. And remember: there are always others in the same situation as you, so seek their support.

Also, be sure to check out the many Facebook groups and Milblogging communities online. There are thousands of military spouses and significant others out there, ready to support you.

"They look ordinary, they lace up just the same, but it's not the boots that matter, it's my soldier in the boots that means the world to me."

— *Unknown*

ARMY CORE VALUES

In the 1990s, the Army officially adopted what have come to be known as the "Seven Army Core Values" and began teaching these values as basic warrior traits. They are arranged with the first letter of each word forming the acronym LDRSHIP (leadership). As a spouse or significant other, it is important to realize early on that soldiers place their Army mission first—they are trained to do so. While your soldier loves you, his first job is to honor and protect the country and fellow comrades. It is the most admirable of traits: putting others' interests ahead of one's own.

The seven Army Core Values[2] are as follows:

Loyalty – Bear true faith and allegiance to the U.S. Constitution, the Army, your unit and other soldiers.

Duty – Fulfill your obligations.

Respect – Treat others as they should be treated.

Selfless Service – Put the welfare of the nation, the Army and your subordinates before your own.

Honor – Live up to Army values.

Integrity – Do what's right, legally and morally.

Personal Courage – Face fear, danger or adversity (physical or moral).

---

[2] "Living the Army Values." U.S. Army. http://www.goArmy.com/soldier-life/being-a-soldier/living-the-Army-values.html.

SOLDIER'S CREED

Army soldiers are trained and encouraged to live and die by the Soldier's Creed, and all enlisted Army personnel are taught the Soldier's Creed during Basic Training. Understanding this creed will help you better relate to the mindset of your significant other or spouse, as well as understand some of the choices he or she makes. The Warrior Ethos, the Army's distinguishing character and guiding beliefs, are incorporated into the Soldier's Creed (see bold print):

I am an American Soldier.
I am a Warrior and a member of a team. I serve the people of the United States and live the Army Values.

I will always place the mission first.
I will never accept defeat.
I will never quit.
I will never leave a fallen comrade.

I am disciplined, physically and mentally tough, trained and proficient in my warrior tasks and drills.
I always maintain my arms, my equipment and myself.
I am an expert and I am a professional.
I stand ready to deploy, engage and destroy the enemies of the United States of America in close combat.
I am a guardian of freedom and the American way of life.
I am an American Soldier.

In addition to the Soldier's Creed, there are creeds based on branch or position. For example, an NCO (non-commissioned officer) has an NCO's Creed, a drill sergeant has a Drill Sergeant's Creed and a U.S. Army Ranger has their own creed.

MILITARY TRAINING AND STRUCTURE

BASIC TRAINING: BUILDING AN ARMY SOLDIER

If your spouse or significant other joins the military after you get together, he or she will have to go to Basic Training. Basic Training, or Boot Camp, is the physical and mental training an individual undergoes to become a soldier in the U.S. Army. It is designed to be highly intensive and challenging, both physically and psychologically.

While it's a challenging time for your soldier, there are a few things you can look forward to. First, your soldier will come home knowing how to fold clothes and take orders from someone else. Second, he or she will probably have a newfound respect for your cooking. See, there are some perks to being a military spouse or significant other!

All jokes aside, understanding what your soldier goes through in Basic Training is important to your introduction to Army life. Basic Training is divided into two parts:

Part I: Basic Combat Training (BCT)

Part II: Advanced Individual Training (AIT)

These typically occur at different locations, but if BCT and AIT are available at the same location, your soldier will attend One Station Unit Training (OSUT) and stay there for the duration of both.

Basic Combat Training (BCT) consists of the first ten weeks of the total Basic Training period. Individuals learn about the fundamentals of being a soldier, from combat techniques to the proper way to address a superior. They undergo rigorous physical training to prepare their bodies for the strain of combat. Self-discipline is also taught in Basic in order to introduce prospective soldiers to a strict daily schedule. The first week consists of the "reception," which is when the recruits are introduced to the Army way of life—they receive uniforms, eat in the chow hall, get a military haircut and get used to an intensely structured schedule.

A graduation ceremony that family members can attend is held at the end of the ten weeks. The mother of a soldier recently told me that her son's Basic Training graduation was one of the best events she has ever attended, and it showcased everything good about the U.S.A. She was filled with pride not only for her son, but for all the men and women celebrating such an amazing accomplishment.

Advanced Individual Training (AIT) consists of the remainder of the total Basic Training period, and this is where recruits train for their chosen MOS (Military Occupational Specialty). An MOS could be something such as a mechanic, intelligence or sharp shooter. These courses last anywhere from six to 52 weeks, depending on the MOS they train in. During AIT, soldiers find out where their upcoming duty stations will be; after graduation, they transfer to their new duty stations.

Basic Training is a shock to the system. Most recruits try not to stand out during this time; they just keep their heads down and get through it.

In order to make things easier on both your soldier and yourself, there are a few things to remember while your soldier is at Basic:

1. His days are completely controlled.

2. He may not have much time to call you during the first ten weeks. This doesn't mean your soldier doesn't care about you or doesn't want to talk to you.

3. Your life together will be put on hold for a while; you must learn to accept this.

4. He will not enjoy the time spent apart from you either, and you must try to be supportive and encouraging, even if it is hard to do so.

5. Your loved one is being broken down, both mentally and physically; the Army does this so they can rebuild him into a soldier. Be patient as your soldier goes through this process.

6. Recruits may express that they've made a mistake in joining the military. This feeling normally goes away after they begin bonding with fellow recruits, reach graduation and have a renewed self-confidence after the completion of training.

7. Everything your soldier receives by mail will be monitored. Don't send letters that smell like perfume or are decorated in a way that superiors will know it is from a girlfriend or spouse.

8. Recruits won't have much space at Basic, so don't send packages filled with items that are difficult to store.

9. Keep in mind that nothing is private. If you send pictures, make sure they are not risqué.

So, why can't you send decorated letters or certain items? What are some other things to expect during Basic? Here are a few stories that will give you a sliver of what life is like for a freshman in the military:

Miranda, the girlfriend of a freshman at West Point Military Academy, told me about her experiences. One time, she sent a letter to her soldier; his superiors could tell it was from his girlfriend, so they made him read the letter out loud…in front of everybody. To avoid this, she learned to change her hand writing and sign the return address with his mother's name. She also had to get used to him hanging up unexpectedly, as something or someone could quickly cause him to have to end the conversation. She learned the hard way what all military spouses learn quickly: you have to be understanding and wait a lot of the time. It's times like these when the personal attribute of patience comes in handy.

When my husband was in Basic Training, recruits who received packages of cookies or brownies were forced by their superiors to sit down and eat the entire amount. Then, they would PT (physical train) them like crazy until they got sick.

The girlfriend of a plebe in Basic said her boyfriend was only allowed to call her three times during the ten weeks of Basic Training—and two of those calls were limited to five minutes.

Soldiers learn to eat fast in Basic Training. When the last one to get his food is done, they're all done. Even today, several years after Basic, my husband doesn't like to talk when he eats. Instead, he gets down to the task at hand—eating!

THE CHAIN OF COMMAND

If you've read the first chapters straight through until now, you're beginning to realize that there is a structure to every aspect of military life. But it doesn't stop there: within the rank structure, soldiers must also follow a ladder of hierarchy, known as the chain of command. For example, if an issue arises, a Private (PV1) would relay the issue to the First Line Leader (E5 or E6); if the issue can't be resolved, the First Line Leader then takes it to their First Line Leader, and so on up the ladder. The chain of command ranks are designed so that orders can be given swiftly and without a question of authority. Understanding this chain of command will help you better understand your soldier's career, as well as help make sense of the strictly structured military lifestyle.

A soldier's acceleration from an enlisted soldier to an officer is dependent upon a combination of variables—primarily, time in grade (rank) and time in service. Time in grade is the amount of time a soldier has spent in his or her current rank, which is associated with a specific pay grade. Time in service refers to how long your soldier has served in the U.S. military. Additional variables are also considered, such as whether he or she holds a college degree or has any additional military training and schooling. Just like any promotion, there are an endless number of variables and regulations taken into account to determine when a soldier gets promoted to the next pay grade and rank. See figure 1 for an explanation of each rank, including insignia, abbreviation and rank/grade.[3]

---

[3] *U.S. Army Board Study Guide.* http://www.armystudyguide.com.

Enlisted personnel are referred to as E1 – E9, with soldiers just starting out in Basic ranked E1, the lowest grade. Warrant officers, "W" grades, range from W1 – W5. Officers, "O" grades range from O1 – O10.

Enlisted Ranks			
Title	**Insignia**	**Abbreviation**	**Rank/Grade**
Private	No Insignia	PV1	E1
Private First Class		PV2	E2
Private First Class		PFC	E3
Specialist		SPC	E4
Corporal		CPL	E4
Sergeant		SGT	E5
Staff Sergeant		SSG	E6
Sergeant First Class		SFC	E7

Figure 1

Enlisted Ranks

Title	Insignia	Abbreviation	Rank/Grade
Master Sergeant		MSG	E8
First Sergeant		1SG	E8
Sergeant Major		SGM	E9
Command Sergeant Major		CSM	E9
Sergeant Major of the Army		SMA	E9

Figure 1

Warrant Officer Ranks

Title	Insignia	Abbreviation	Rank/Grade
Warrant Officer		WO1	W-1
Chief Warrant Officer		WO2	W-2
Chief Warrant Officer		WO3	W-3
Chief Warrant Officer		WO4	W-4
Chief Warrant Officer		WO5	W-5

Figure 1

Officer Ranks

Title	Insignia	Abbreviation	Rank/Grade
Second Lieutenant		2LT	O1
First Lieutenant		1LT	O2
Captain		CPT	O3
Major		MAJ	O4
Lieutenant Colonel		LTC	O5
Colonel		COL	O6

Figure 1

Officer Ranks

Title	Insignia	Abbreviation	Rank/Grade
Brigadier General	★	BG	O7
Major General	★★	MG	O8
Lieutenant General	★★★	LTG	O9
General	★★★★	GEN	O10
General of the Army	★★★★★	GOA	

Figure 1

As if there isn't enough to learn with just the ranks and titles, you'll find that most soldiers are called three to four different names—none of which are their first names. They're either referred to by last name, rank, nickname or title (XO, Top, 1st sergeant). The nicknames are great: Crazy Eye, Torso, Crusty, Ginger.

You'll be introduced to Army colleagues by their first names, though, so it can get confusing. My husband and I use personal encounters or stories to communicate about individuals; this helps us decipher who we are referencing, since he refers to titles and I normally know first names.

RESOURCE

To view a 2012 list of Army pay, based on rank, please visit: http://www.militaryfactory.com/2012-military-pay-chart.asp.

FRATERNIZATION: HOW RANK AFFECTS YOU AND YOUR SOLDIER

There are rules for soldiers, and unwritten rules for spouses, regarding "fraternization," which just means associating with others in a social manner. Let's take a brief look at what is expected so you know where your soldier fits into the social spectrum. Learning these rules now will help you avoid embarrassing faux pas, as well as prepare you for social life in the military.

Soldiers

While on post, higher-ranking soldiers are highly discouraged from associating with lower-ranking soldiers, in order to avoid favoritism. This is the reason for separate neighborhoods (officer neighborhoods and enlisted neighborhoods) on a military installation. This fraternization rule applies more to Active Duty soldiers than to Reserve or National Guard, since Active Duty soldiers most often live on base, making it much easier to enforce.

Spouses

Maybe you've watched the HBO series, *Army Wives*, and have seen how women relate to one another on post. While I enjoy watching the show, it is not always the most accurate representation of military relationships.

The same rule for soldiers applies somewhat to spouses. It is assumed that spouses of higher-ranking military personnel will know things that shouldn't be told to spouses of lower-ranking military personnel and therefore shouldn't communicate on a social level. There is no hard and fast rule on this, but it is something to be aware of. Again, since families of Reserve or National Guard soldiers live off base, the socialization rules are not as strictly enforced.

Katie, a seasoned Army wife, told me she never felt snubbed by officers' wives when her husband was enlisted. But, when her husband went from being an enlisted soldier one day to an officer the next, the enlisted women withdrew their friendship. It was hard to make the sudden switch from being an enlisted soldier's wife to an officer's wife, and her friendships suffered as a result.

As a spouse, you need to remember that your soldier earned his rank, not you. It is best to be polite and courteous to every spouse, regardless of their soldier's rank.

Many military spouses are highly educated, well-traveled men and women with professional backgrounds. A good rule of thumb is to not judge anyone until you get to know them.

DIFFERENCES BETWEEN ACTIVE DUTY, RESERVE AND ARMY NATIONAL GUARD

I can't tell you how many times I asked my husband how the Army was organized. "Okay," I'd say to him, "you're deploying and *what* group are you in and *who else* is going and *what* are their jobs?" Since there are variations between the various components of the U.S. Army for Active Duty, Reserve and National Guard, it can be hard to understand the differences.

So, what are the differences between Active Duty, Reserve and National Guard? This is where things get a little tricky. Trying to explain how promotions, deployments and benefits operate is difficult, as each component of the Army functions slightly differently. Let's look at a brief overview of each:

Active Duty
Federally regulated
+ Soldiers work for the U.S. Army as their full-time jobs.
+ Soldiers train for and maintain operational readiness every day of the year.
+ Families live on or near an Army installation.
+ Soldiers are the first to be deployed for an operation or conflict.

+ Soldiers and families have access to a support network and perks like base amenities, events, commissary and discount offers.

Reserve

Federally regulated

+ Reservists work a *minimum* of one weekend a month and two weeks a year.
+ Reservists are citizen soldier volunteers who have civilian jobs during the week.
+ Reservists are deployed when called upon by the federal government.
+ Families live off base.
+ Soldiers and families don't have the same support network or perks as readily available as Active Duty for things such as base amenities, events, commissary and discount offers.
+ Some soldiers live hours away from a military base, and many families don't have the support of a military community during deployments.

National Guard

Primarily state regulated

+ National Guardsmen work a *minimum* of one weekend a month and two weeks a year.
+ The National Guard is primarily regulated by the governor of its state.

- National Guardsmen are citizen soldier volunteers who have civilian jobs during the week.
- A soldier can be considered on Active Duty status while in the National Guard. (Someone needs to keep it running between the one weekend a month and two weeks a year!)
- Guardsmen are deployed when called upon by the state *or* federal government. The president is able to ask the state governor for the troops to mobilize when needed.
- Families live off base.
- Soldiers and families don't have the same support network or perks as readily available as Active Duty for things such as base amenities, events, commissary and discount offers.
- Some soldiers live hours away from a military base, and many families don't have the support of a military community during deployments.

 If your soldier is in the Reserve or National Guard, he may make less money during a deployment than if working his civilian job. Plan ahead for this situation, as deployments are inevitable.

Figure 2 details the structure of the United States Army for both the Active Duty Army and the Army National Guard. It will give you a basic idea of where your soldier falls in the spectrum, as well as who they report to in the chain of command. The Army Reserve is led by the Chief, Army Reserve who then falls under the Secretary of the Army.

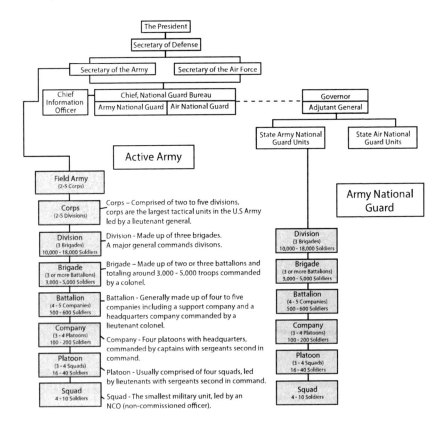

Figure 2

UNIFORMS: A SOLDIER'S RESUME

Unlike civilians, soldiers literally wear their resumes on their uniforms. By merely looking at a photograph of my friend's Green Beret soldier in uniform, my husband was able to tell me how many years of combat experience he had. When I asked how he could tell, he told me it was on the soldier's arm. It kind of gives a new meaning to wearing your heart on your sleeve—only, instead of displaying emotions, it's military status and experience that is displayed for the world to see.

As a matter of fact, soldiers have a manual that tells them exactly how to wear their Army uniforms and insignia and even how to groom themselves; it is all spelled out in the *Wear and Appearance of Army Uniforms and Insignia*, the regulation AR 670-1 manual. Yes, the Army has a 337 page manual, which dictates how soldiers' uniforms should appear and fit; when and where uniforms can be worn; how jewelry should be worn; what maternity work uniforms are available; and when civilian clothes can be worn, among other regulations. Remember: the Army has structure to every process...even getting dressed.

There are currently three main Army uniforms: Army Combat Uniform, Army Service Uniform and Army Blues. Each uniform is to be worn in specific situations, and each of the Army's service dress uniforms has a specific manner of wear, based on the soldier's rank. In each of the following photos, the soldier is "standing at attention," which means he is standing straight, head forward, chest up, stomach in, arms at his sides with closed fists, thumb forward and palms along the seams of his pants. Now, that's structure!

ARMY COMBAT UNIFORM (ACU)

Rank Insignia

Patrol Cap

Name Tape

Current Unit Patch

U.S. Flag

Rank Insignia

Deployed Unit Patch
(unit patch service member deployed with)

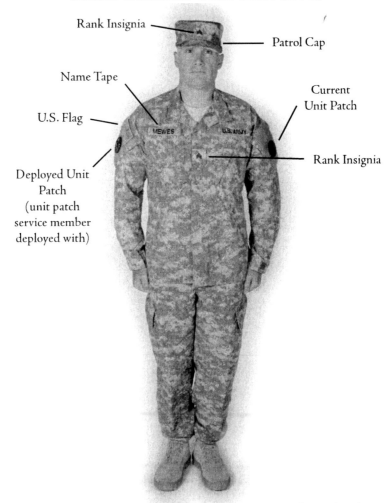

The Army Combat Uniform is worn in garrison (home base) and combat zones.

ARMY SERVICE UNIFORM (ASU)
ARMY GREENS, CLASS A

Beret — Distinctive Unit Insignia

U.S. Gold Lapel Disc — Enlisted Branch Gold Lapel Disc (related to field)

Distinctive Unit Insignia — Distinctive Unit Insignia

Regimental Crest (related to field, i.e. mechanic, special forces) — Unit Patch

Unit Awards — Service Ribbons
Name Plate —

Chevrons (rank insignia) — Qualification Bars & Badges

Service Stripes (years in service)

Oxford Shoes

The Army Greens are slowly being replaced by the Army Blues as the Army Service Uniform (ASU) to be used for formal occasions, such as a Cavalry Ball or a wedding, but Army Greens are still in use until October 2015.

ARMY SERVICE UNIFORM (ASU) – ARMY BLUES

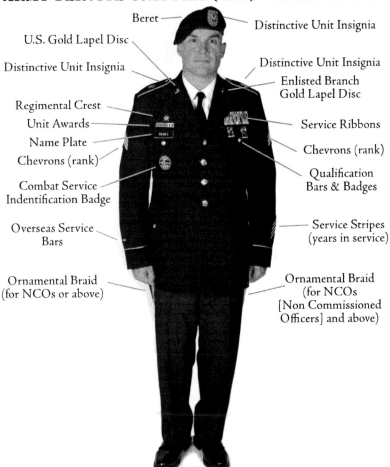

Beret

Distinctive Unit Insignia

U.S. Gold Lapel Disc

Distinctive Unit Insignia

Distinctive Unit Insignia

Enlisted Branch
Gold Lapel Disc

Regimental Crest

Unit Awards

Name Plate

Chevrons (rank)

Service Ribbons

Chevrons (rank)

Qualification
Bars & Badges

Combat Service
Indentification Badge

Overseas Service
Bars

Service Stripes
(years in service)

Ornamental Braid
(for NCOs or above)

Ornamental Braid
(for NCOs
[Non Commissioned
Officers] and above)

Army Blues are becoming the new standard ASU (Army Service Uniform)
to be used for formal occasions, such as a Cavalry Ball or wedding.
The Army Blues must be worn Army-wide for these types of events
as mandatory wear after October 2015.

INSIGNIA

An insignia is a badge showing office or rank. Army insignia was designed in the Continental Army era so that one could tell the difference between a commissioned officer and private. The Army wanted a badge of distinction to separate one from another.

Today, there are different insignia badges and patches for each field of the Army. Learning the most common insignias will help you better understand your loved one's job, as well as the jobs of fellow soldiers. See the images on the following for a few examples of Army insignia.

RESOURCE

Learn more about Army uniforms, insignia and regulations at http://www.military.com/benefits/resources/Army-uniform.

Samples of Branch Insignia

Christian Chaplain

Infantry

Corps of Engineers

Medical Corps

Military Intelligence

Army Band

COINS

A coin can also be a part of your soldier's uniform. The history of the coin can't be confirmed, but legend says that it began in WWI, when an Army Air Corps lieutenant ordered bronze medallions with his company's insignia on them. He then presented one coin to pilots in his squadron as a memento of their service together.

The story continues that one of the pilots put it around his neck for safe keeping before flying out on a mission. This pilot was shot down and captured by the Germans, who took everything from his pockets, but left the coin around his neck. He later escaped from the Germans and made contact with a French patrol. He had no way to identify himself to the Frenchman as an American (rather than a German) without his ID, so he showed the Frenchman the coin medallion. The French patrolman recognized his coin and was able to prove his identity before he was executed. When he returned back to his squadron, it became mandatory for all members to carry a coin with them.

Back then, in order to mandate that coins were always carried, pilots would challenge each other to produce their coins. If someone didn't produce the coin, he was required to buy a drink for the challenger. If he could produce the coin, he would be treated to a drink from the challenger.

Today, coins are given to Army soldiers to signify outstanding achievement or membership in a particular unit.

Call for Coins (Challenging)

Similar to the old Army tradition, today's Army practices an informal "Call for Coins." When this occurs, there is a call for a throw down of coins, and the soldier with the highest-ranking coin buys the other person a drink. Each unit has different challenges, though. For example, my husband's sergeant major gave everyone in his unit a coin. If he calls for coins and someone can't product his coin, the sergeant major requires that person to buy him a soda.

Some sample coins are shown on the following page.

If you do your soldier's laundry and find a military coin in his or her pocket, be sure to put it back after doing the wash. If you don't, your soldier may have to buy everyone a round of drinks!

Front Side

Back Side

MILITARY TIME: THE 24-HOUR CLOCK

The military uses a 24-hour clock, which was originally created to avoid confusion when communicating times. So, instead of 4:00 a.m., it would be 0400. Some military personnel talk only in military time, while others waver back and forth between civilian and military. And while many National Guard members will speak in civilian time when they're not on the military base, they may come home speaking in military language after a drill weekend or deployment.

Once, when my husband said we needed to be at a party by 1815, I told him to tell me in "real" time so I'd understand. I later learned to count in my head or on my fingers to figure it out. I do this by mentally starting with noon (1200) and then counting up on my fingers—1300, 1400 and so on—to figure it out. If your spouse says you need to be at a party by 2030, would you get there on time? If you planned to arrive at 8:30 p.m., great job. You are correct!

Calendar dates are also written differently in the military. Instead of the traditional month/day/year, the military writes it day/month/year. For example, 14/8/2011, or 14 August 2011, is the same as August 14, 2011. This can be especially confusing with lower numbered months and days, such as 01/3/2011, which is the same as March 1, 2011.

Military = Civilian	Military = Civilian
0001 = 12:01 am	1300 = 1:00 pm
0100 = 1:00 am	1400 = 2:00 pm
0200 = 2:00 am	1500 = 3:00 pm
0300 = 3:00 am	1600 = 4:00 pm
0400 = 4:00 am	1700 = 5:00 pm
0500 = 5:00 am	1800 = 6:00 pm
0600 = 6:00 am	1900 = 7:00 pm
0700 = 7:00 am	2000 = 8:00 pm
0800 = 8:00 am	2100 = 9:00 pm
0900 = 9:00 am	2200 = 10:00 pm
1000 = 10:00 am	2300 = 11:00 pm
1100 = 11:00 am	2400 = 12 Midnight
1200 = Noon	

How to Say It...

0100 (1:00 a.m.) = zero one hundred hours
0700 (7:00 a.m.) = zero seven hundred hours
0230 (2:30 a.m.) = zero two thirty hours
1300 (1:00 p.m.) = thirteen hundred hours
1815 (6:15 p.m.) = eighteen fifteen hours

THE ALPHA-BRAVO-CHARLIES: ABCS OF THE MILITARY ALPHABET

The military alphabet is frequently used in pop culture: you'll hear movie stars communicate orders on the big screen with phrases like, "Bravo-Tango-Whiskey-Zulu." Unless you know military lingo, you might not notice how often it's used. Before my own intro to Army life, I used to think they just made those words up; now, I know they were using the military alphabet all along.

Every branch of the military uses what is called the phonetic alphabet. This helps distinguish similar-sounding letters, like B, T, D and P, during high-stress combat situations or phone conversations. Instead, if you say words like, "Bravo," "Tango," "Delta," and "Papa," the person on the other end of the order will understand the message, and the likelihood of an error is significantly decreased.

Let's take a look at the military alphabet:

A	Alpha	**N**	November
B	Bravo	**O**	Oscar
C	Charlie	**P**	Papa
D	Delta	**Q**	Quebec
E	Echo	**R**	Romeo
F	Foxtrot	**S**	Sierra
G	Golf	**T**	Tango
H	Hotel	**U**	Uniform
I	India	**V**	Victor
J	Juliet	**W**	Whiskey
K	Kilo	**X**	X-ray
L	Lima	**Y**	Yankee
M	Mike	**Z**	Zulu

Can you decode the message below?

India Lima Oscar Victor Echo Mike Yankee Sierra Oscar Lima Delta India Echo Romeo.[4]

---

[4] If you guessed, "I love my soldier," you got it! Good work.

OMG: ACRONYMS AND OTHER STRANGE WORDS

OMG, there are hundreds of acronyms used in the Army. Soldiers seem to have acronyms for everything and use them as if everyone around them understands what they mean. Most of the time, they honestly don't even know they're using "military speak"; because of this, it's best to learn some of the more common acronyms so the two of you can somewhat speak the same language.

I love to tell the story of when my husband told me he had to go to HRO. I asked, "What is HRO?" He looked at me strangely and replied that it was the Human Resources Office. Later, he said he thought I was joking when I asked him what HRO was, because it was so obvious. Well, we civilians just call it HR…right?

To help you avoid similar situations, I've included a list of the top 25 acronyms you should know when entering the Army lifestyle. You will hear many, many more over the years, and you will even start speaking in acronyms yourself. Soon you'll impress your soldier with your new terminology.

Top 25 Military Acronyms

1. **AAFES:** Army and Air Force Exchange Service – An organization of the Department of Defense (DoD) that provides merchandise and services in the post exchange (PX) at lower prices to those with a military ID card.

2. **ACU:** Active Combat Uniform – The current combat uniform worn by the United States Army.

3. **BAH:** Basic Allowance for Housing – The allowance for soldiers living off post, based on geographic location.

4. **CHU** (pronounced "Chew"): Containerized Housing Unit or Combat Housing Unit – What soldiers sleep in most often while deployed; their home away from home.

5. **CO:** Commanding Officer – Officer in command of a military unit.

6. **DEERS:** Defense Enrollment Eligibility Reporting System – A database of uniformed services members, their family members and those eligible for military benefits, including TRICARE. See page 85 for more information.

7. **DFAC:** Dining Facility (also referred to as the "chow hall") – This is where soldiers go to eat; it is like their cafeteria.

8. **DFAS:** Defense Finance and Accounting Services – Provides payment services to the United States Department of Defense.

9. **DoD:** Department of Defense – The U.S. federal government branch that is responsible for ensuring our military is adequate in protecting our national security.

10. **FOB:** Forward Operating Base – This is the "home base" position for deployed soldiers and is used to support tactical operations in the field.

11. **FRG:** Family Readiness Group – A command-sponsored organization of family members, volunteers and soldiers belonging to a unit, which together provide an avenue of mutual support and assistance, as well as a network of communications between a soldier's family members, the chain of command and community resources.

12. **JAG:** Judge Advocate General – A group of Army officers who are lawyers; they provide a range of legal services to soldiers in the U.S. Army.

13. **LES:** Leave and Earnings Statement – The military pay stub. See page 91 for more information.

14. **MFLC:** Military Family Life Consultants – A group that provides anonymous and confidential counseling assistance to soldiers and their family members.

15. **MOS:** Military Occupational Specialty – What the Army uses to identify specific jobs such as; mechanic, interpreter, cook, special operations engineer.

16. **MWR:** Morale, Welfare and Recreation – An organization that provides a network of support and leisure services to enhance the lives of soldiers, civilians, families and military retirees.

17. **OPSEC:** Operational Security – The process of making sure military information is secure and does not get into the hands of those who could use it to harm our soldiers or country. See page 141 for more information.

18. **PCS:** Permanent Change of Station – Moving from one duty station to another; referred to as PCSing.

19. **POA:** Power of Attorney – Written authorization to represent or act on another's behalf in private affairs, business and other legal matters.

20. **PX:** Post Exchange – A retail store operating on U.S. military installations.

21. **PT:** Physical Training – How Army soldiers refer to exercise and working out.

22. **R&R:** Slang in the military for rest and recuperation/relaxation, otherwise referred to as "leave."

23. **TDY:** Temporary Duty – A change in location from a soldiers permanent duty station to a temporary duty station, usually lasting no longer than six months.

24. **TSP:** Thrift Savings Plan – A contribution retirement savings plan for federal employees.

25. **XO:** Executive Officer – Officer in charge of the daily functional operations of a unit.

In addition to the myriad of acronyms, there are also some strange words you may want to familiarize yourself with as your soldier will use them regularly.

Chow – Military slang for food. Soldiers will say they are going to the "chow hall" to eat.

HOOAH! – Heard, Understood and Acknowledged. Commonly used when shouting out a response cheer. For example, a sergeant may bark orders and then say, "Do you understand, soldier?" The private's response would be, "HOOAH, Sir!"

Roger – This simply means, "yes."

While FRAGO may not be the most commonly used acronym, it is one of the most important. A FRAGO (Fragmentary Order) in the military is a hasty or sudden change or amendment to a previous operational order. Remember: things change fast in the Army; be ready to accept and embrace change.

RESOURCES

- If you'd like to add to your repertoire, check out the official Department of Defense "Dictionary of Military and Associated Terms" at www.dtic.mil/doctrine/dod_dictionary/

- Or, if you want to learn military slang, check out the Wiktionary glossary at http://en.wiktionary.org/wiki/Appendix:Glossary_of_military_slang

BENEFITS AND PAY

DEERS: THE MILITARY DATABASE

As discussed earlier, DEERS is an acronym that stands for Defense Enrollment Eligibility Reporting System. As a military spouse or significant other, neither you nor your dependents will be eligible for TRICARE until you are entered into the DEERS system. Translated, that means that, until you're entered into DEERS, you're not eligible for insurance benefits.

DEERS supports benefit delivery for medical, dental, education and life insurance. Your sponsor (i.e., your soldier) must enroll you and your dependents into DEERS, unless you have a power of attorney. When registering, he or she must provide the original copies of a birth certificate and social security card for any dependents being enrolled. If you have recently married, be sure to supply an original copy of your marriage certificate.

In addition to handling benefits, DEERS is responsible for producing DoD military ID cards. With a military dependent ID card, you will be able to:

- Receive military discounts at participating businesses (10 percent is average)

- Enter a military post without providing your driver's license and proof of insurance (each base has varying entry requirements)

- Shop at the PX (post exchange)

- Shop at the commissary

- Use USO services when traveling

- Fill up your car with gas on a military post

- Rent sporting equipment from MWR (Morale, Welfare and Recreation)

- …and many more advantages only available to card-carrying members of the military; guard this card carefully!

All family members over the age of 10 must have a military ID card.

RESOURCES

- If you need to change or update your information due to a new baby or a marriage, you can do it onsite; locate a Rapids site (a military registration location) near you by visiting http://www.dmdc.osd.mil/rsl/ appj/

- Changes or updates can also be done online via the DEERS website, http://tricare.mil/mybenefit/home/overview/ Eligibility/DEERS

TRICARE INSURANCE BENEFITS

TRICARE is the health care program serving Active Duty, National Guard and Reserve members, retirees and their families through the DoD (Department of Defense). It functions slightly differently in that doctors may be assigned to you, and the benefits are much better than in the private sector. Hallelujah!

TRICARE offers a number of benefit plans, and the company is separated into three main geographic regions: north, south and west.

This region separation can be tricky. When my husband and I initially called TRICARE to find out the fax number to submit my enrollment paperwork after we were married, we were given the incorrect fax number—TriNorth instead of TriWest. When we realized we'd submitted the paperwork to the incorrect region, we tried to remedy it by having TriNorth fax the application to TriWest. Surprisingly, the two regions do not talk to each other, could not fax my application to each other and could not get on a conference call to confirm that TriNorth did receive enrollment information on time. My numerous attempts to rectify the situation and resubmit my paperwork to TriWest were unsuccessful. TRICARE ended up giving us the run around for an entire month, until the monthly enrollment cycle (the 20th of each month) restarted. After a month of red tape and time-intensive phone calls, I was finally entered correctly into the TriWest region. Lesson learned.

Health Plan Options

TRICARE offers several different health plan options for military families, which depend on location and if the military service member is Active Duty, deployed, Reserve or retired. TRICARE Prime and Prime Remote are the most common options. Prime Remote is for Active Duty service members living 50 miles or an hour drive time away from a MTF (military treatment facility). When you enroll in TRICARE, you will be assigned a primary care manager (PCM), either at an MTF or from the TRICARE network of doctors and physicians. Your PCM will refer you to a specialist (such as a dermatologist, an OBGYN, an eye doctor, etc.) for any care he or she cannot provide and will coordinate with your regional TRICARE contractor for authorizations, find specialists you may need in the regional TRICARE network and file claims on your behalf. When the process goes smoothly, there is nothing like TRICARE benefits. They are amazing compared to civilian benefits.

But while the benefits are great, dealing with TRICARE can be difficult. For this reason, I have included some tips to deal with TRICARE. Be sure to cover all your bases ahead of time to minimize frustrations or unexpected out-of-pocket expenses.

Tips for Dealing with TRICARE:

1. When enrolling, be sure to submit your TRICARE application on or before the 20th of the month, as benefits are effective the first day of the following month.

2. Call back to confirm your enrollment or referral after submitting your paperwork. Don't ever assume TRICARE received it or that it was processed correctly...learn from my mistake on this one.

3. You will be assigned a primary care manager (PCM) from TRICARE. In some instances, you may select yours. Before my husband deployed, we were assigned a PCM that didn't accept Prime Remote. So, we had to find a new one, confirm our selection with TRICARE and be sure it was entered into their system before going to the doctor.

4. Confirm that you have a referral from your PCM before making an appointment with a specialist. TRICARE takes five to seven business days to process a referral, so plan ahead and then confirm it was received and processed before going to your appointment. Otherwise, you might pay out-of-pocket for the visit.

5. Remember: your soldier is considered your sponsor; you will be identified by his or her social security number in the military and through TRICARE.

RESOURCE

Your TRICARE options and benefits are best explained at the TRICARE website, www.TRICARE.mil.

UNDERSTANDING AN LES, AKA PAY STUB

A Leave and Earning Statement (LES) is the equivalent of a civilian pay stub. You will need to learn how to read an LES, because it contains vital information regarding your soldier's income, leave, combat pay, state and federal tax, housing allowance (BAH) and more. Plus, you need to know how much money your soldier makes in order to spend it… right? All kidding aside, learn how to read this because you may be the one managing the finances while your spouse is deployed.

Your soldier can only access his or her LES online through the myPay website (see "Resources" at the end of this chapter); you are able to log in with his or her username and password to monitor it for accuracy. This is a good idea during a deployment, since you won't receive hard copies in the mail. Soldiers can use myPay to print their W2 or view military pay charts, military benefits and retirement benefits. A sample Active Duty LES has been included (see figure 3), although an LES is slightly different for National Guard and Reserve soldiers. On the myPay website, you can also:

+ Change federal and state tax withholdings

+ Print travel vouchers

+ Update electronic funds transfer information

+ Control Thrift Savings Plan (TSP) enrollments

Sample Active Duty LES Statement (Fig 3)

DEFENSE FINANCE AND ACCOUNTING SERVICE MILITARY LEAVE AND EARNINGS STATEMENT									
ID	NAME (LAST, FIRST, MI) 1	SOC SEC NO 2	GRADE 3	PAY DATE 4	YRS SVC 5	ETS 6	BRANCH 7	ADSN/DSSN 8	PERIOD COVERED 9

ENTITLEMENTS		DEDUCTIONS		ALLOTMENTS		SUMMARY	
TYPE	AMOUNT	TYPE	AMOUNT	TYPE	AMOUNT	+ AMT FWD	13
A B C D E F G H i j K L M N O	10	11		12		+ TOT ENT	14
						- TOT DED	15
						- TOT ALMT	16
						= NET AMT	17
						- CR FWD	18
						= EOM PAY	19
						DIEMS 23	RET PLAN 24
TOTAL	20		21		22		

LEAVE	BF BAL 25	ERND 26	USED 27	CR BAL 28	ETS BAL 29	LV LOST 30	LV PAID 31	USE/LOSE 32	FED TAXES	WAGE PERIOD 33	WAGE YTD 34	M/S 35	EX 36	ADD'L TAX 37	TAX YTD 38
FICA TAXES	WAGE PERIOD 39	SOC WAGE YTD 40	SOC TAX YTD 41	MED WAGE YTD 42	MED-TAX YTD 43		STATE TAXES	ST 44	WAGE PERIOD 45	WAGE YTD 46	M/S 47	EX 48	TAX YTD 49	
PAY DATA	BAQ TYPE 50	BAQ DEPN 51	VHA ZIP 52	RENT AMT 53	SHARE 54	STAT 55	JFTR 56	DEPNS 57	2D JFTR 58	BAS TYPE 59	CHARITY YTD 60	TPC 61	PACIDN 62	

Thrift Savings Plan (TSP)	BASE PAY RATE 63	BASE PAY CURRENT 64	SPEC PAY RATE 65	SPEC PAY CURRENT 66	INC PAY RATE 67	INC PAY CURRENT 68	BONUS PAY RATE 69	BONUS PAY CURRENT 70
	CURRENTLY NOT USED 71	TSP YTD DEDUCTIONS 72	DEFERRED 73	EXEMPT 74	CURRENTLY NOT USED 75			

REMARKS   YTD ENTITLE_____   YTD DEDUCT _____

76   77   78

www.dfas.mil

DFAS Form 702, Jan 02

Figure 3 shows a sample LES. The following is a brief description of the information contained in each range of numbered fields, although more detailed information can be found online.

1 – 9:   Soldier identification information

10 – 24:   Entitlements, deductions, allotments, their respective totals, a mathematical summary portion, date initially entered military service and retirement plan

25 – 32:   Leave information

33 – 38:   Federal tax withholding information

39 – 43:   Federal Insurance Contributions Act (FICA) information

44 –49:   State tax information

50 – 62:   Additional information, such as the number and type of dependents, amount of rent being paid and zip code used for the housing allowance

63 – 75:   Thrift Savings Plan (TSP) information

76:   Additional remarks from varying levels of command, as well as the literal explanation of starts, stops and changes to pay items in the entries within the entitlements, deductions and allotments sections

77:   Total yearly entitlements

78:   Total deductions for the calendar year

Service members serving outside of the United States are eligible to receive a tax extension during a deployment. For guides and tips on taxes, visit the Military.com tax center.

- To access your soldier's LES, visit https://mypay.dfas.mil/mypay.aspx.

- For questions regarding an LES, contact your local disbursing/finance office.

- A good resource on how to read an LES can be found on the Defense Finance and Accounting Services website, http://www.dfas.mil/dfas/militarymembers/payentitlements/aboutpay.html.

BASE RULES: WHAT NO ONE TELLS YOU AHEAD OF TIME

Depending on your specific situation, there are base rules that need to be followed…and ignorance of these rules won't fly as an excuse. It's best to learn them ahead of time; it will save you and your soldier embarrassment, as well as show respect for the Army lifestyle. Regardless of whether your soldier's base is Army, Navy, Air Force or Marine (and as a National Guardsman, he or she could be stationed at any), there are codes of conduct, etiquette and procedures you need to follow while on a military installation.

Be sure to check the rules specific to the base you frequent, as these rules may vary. Included are general guidelines to follow:

General Base Rules

- **Entering a Base:** Anybody driving onto a military base must have the appropriate DoD (Department of Defense) sticker, base permit/pass, contractor ID card (if applicable), valid driver's license and proof of registration and insurance. All visitors must register at the base gate and obtain a temporary visitor's pass, as well as pass a vehicle inspection, in order to drive on base. After you're married, you become a military dependent and need to acquire the DoD decal for your car. This, along with a military ID card, will get you right through security. On a National Guard base, you will typically need a driver's license and proof of insurance, and your soldier may need to call ahead to let them know you're coming to ensure the process is quick and easy. Note: Decals may not be required at your base anymore as the rules are in flux at this time.

- **Colors Salute:** Every morning and night, the U.S. flag is raised and lowered on military bases and a patriotic song may be played. This is known as "Colors," which refers to the United States flag. When the Colors Salute is initiated, military personnel stop what they're doing, if possible, come to attention, face the flag and salute. If you hear the music while driving, protocol calls for you to pull over until the music ends. If you can't hear the music, but see other cars pulling over, do the same. Don't pass them, or speed by, as it is considered rude.

- **Walking on Base:** As tempting as it is, don't take shortcuts! You must use the sidewalks; pedestrians are not allowed to walk on the grass, unless it is in a park.

- **Driving near soldiers:** When driving past marching or running soldiers, you must drive under 10 mph.

- **Cell Phone Use:** You may not use a cell phone while driving a motor vehicle on base, although hands-free devices are acceptable on some installations. Each military base has its own specific protocol for enforcing this rule, as well as different consequences for violating it.

Unspoken Etiquette

- **Military personnel rarely show PDA (public displays of affection) in uniform.** As a newly engaged couple, I wanted to hold my soldier's hand and kiss him while on base, but my attempts were met with him putting a lot of distance between us. Needless to say, my feelings were hurt, until he explained that it's not appropriate to show physical affection in uniform. Typically, the only exceptions to this are during a homecoming or deployment ceremony.

- **Military personnel salute officers or higher-ranking soldiers.** I speak from personal experience: walk on the left side of your soldier to avoid being elbowed in the face when he or she salutes higher-ranking officials!

- **Military personnel cannot eat while walking in uniform.** Well, they can, but etiquette says they should not.

You are a reflection of your spouse or family member while on post, whether you like it or not. What you wear and how you act is silently noticed by those around you. Remember, you want your soldier to look professional and competent to higher-ranking officials and their spouses, and your behavior plays a large role in making this happen.

HOLIDAYS & OBSERVANCES

Veterans and Active Duty service members alike appreciate acknowledgement of their sacrifice and service to our great country on patriotic days. While there are specific holidays for each branch of the military, included is a list of holidays and observances celebrated by the federal government and the Army.

April Month of the Military Child
May Military Appreciation Month Armed Forces Day, observed the third Saturday in May Memorial Day, observed the last Monday in May
June D-Day, June 6th Flag Day/Army birthday, June 14th
July Independence Day, July 4th

September

Patriot Day, September 11th

November

Month of the Military Family

Veteran's Day, November 11th

December

Pearl Harbor Remembrance Day, December 7th

R&R: WHEN WILL I SEE MY SOLDIER AGAIN?

Because of all the structure, uncertainty and difficulty in Army life, time off is well-deserved and appreciated by both soldiers and their families. Rest and recuperation (R&R), usually referred to as leave, is basically the same as vacation time. Active Duty soldiers accrue 2.5 days of paid leave per month, which totals 30 paid days per year. Not bad, right? This is way better than in the private sector, where you're lucky to receive two weeks paid vacation a year. And while 30 days might sound like a lot, it can seem short—long periods of separation can be difficult, so make the most of the time you have to spend together.

Of note is that members of the Reserve and National Guard are only eligible to participate in leave, or R&R programs, if they are serving on Active Duty or are in Active Duty training for a period of 30 or more consecutive days.

It's not hard to find things to do on vacation, but if you live overseas, this is an exceptional time to explore your surroundings and soak up a different culture. The military affords families the ability to travel, and by taking advantage of every opportunity given to you, you are so called "licking the spoon of life"!

I was thankful that my colleague, Anna, told me about the Family and Medical Leave Act (FMLA), which allows for unpaid time off for spouses, surrounding military injuries, deployments and leave, without losing their jobs. Visit their FAQs page at http://www.dol.gov/whd/fmla/finalrule/militaryfaqs.pdf, as some restrictions apply. It is great to know the legal benefits you have as a military spouse.

PERKS OF MILITARY TRAVEL

So, your soldier has up to 30 days off per year...but what are you going to do with all that time? Lucky for you, traveling with a military ID offers special privileges. Not only do you have access to nearly any military base around the world from each branch of the military, but you are also able to receive military discounts at certain businesses (we'll get to that next)! Included are a few travel perks you can take advantage of as a military family:

Airplane Hopping – Military "hops" enable qualified soldiers and family members to fly on a military aircraft from one base to another. Although there is normally no cost, it is a very unpredictable form of travel. For this reason, it's recommended that airplane hopping is only used for leisure trips when you are not on a time schedule. View travel options at www.military-hops.com or www.takeahop.com.

Military-Only Resorts – There are resorts around the world only for military personnel. A few of them include: Edelweiss Lodge and Resort in the Bavarian Alps; Armed Forces Recreation Center in Virginia Beach; Hale Koa Hotel in Honolulu, Hawaii; Shades of Green in Orlando; and Florida and Dragon Hill Lodge in Seoul, South Korea. Search online for these resort names to view rates and amenities information. This is a great option for those who like to travel on a budget.

On-Base Lodging – Temporary lodging is available on most military bases for Active Duty, Reserve and National Guard soldiers. Each base varies in cost and accommodations, but you are typically able to rent base housing with a military ID. This makes it extremely convenient while traveling, especially on a budget. For several resources, as well as an overview of where and how to book your travel, visit www.military.com/Travel/Content1/0,,ML_onbase,00.html.

Condo Timeshares – The Armed Forces Vacation Club (AFVC) offers discounted vacations to military families at resorts around the world. Search for vacations available within a specific date range at www.veteransholidays.com/army-vacation-resorts.html.

Discounted Hotels – The Army has a program called the Lodging Success Program (LSP), which offers special rates for hotels located near Army installations. View participating hotels at www.armymwr.com/travel/offdutytravel/default.aspx.

I especially like the Guide to Military Travel website, www.guidetomilitarytravel.com. It has a discount map, which allows you to click on a state to view military discounts in that area. The site also has a downloadable travel checklist to help you prepare for plane and car trips.

RESOURCE

If you are traveling with kids, a great resource is Delicious Baby, which has lists of travel toys for all ages to keep your kids occupied. Genius! Visit www.deliciousbaby.com/products/travel-toys.

USO SERVICES

Believe it or not, another travel perk is access to USO services. When I think of the USO (United Service Organization), images of Bob Hope and WWII pinup girls entertaining the troops come to mind. The organization was created in 1941 in response to a request from President Franklin D. Roosevelt to provide morale, welfare and recreational services to U.S. military personnel and their families. I was pleasantly surprised to discover that the USO is still very active today, and I was especially happy to learn that it can be a huge support to soldiers and their families while traveling.

There are USO centers in many airports around the world for military personnel and their families. These are very important to soldiers and during intensive layovers while traveling on leave, PCSing (changing duty stations) or deploying. Heck, with a military ID, you can use them even if your flight to get away for the weekend is delayed. The organization provides amenities such as bunk beds, bedding, wake up calls, phone usage, showers, airport shuttles, toiletries and free WiFi, along with a computer room, TV room, family room with cribs and toys and complimentary coffee and snacks. As a bonus, the volunteers staffing them are always kind and friendly.

When my husband deployed, volunteers from the USO were at the deployment ceremony at 5:30 a.m. (I mean, 0530!) to give me a hug, wipe away my tears and serve hot coffee and snacks. They made a difficult situation a little bit better. Most volunteers are veterans and understand all too well what soldiers, spouses and their families experience during these stressful situations. Take advantage of what the USO has to offer.

 Locate USO centers around the world when you're traveling by visiting www.uso.org/centers/locate-a-center.aspx.

PCSing: HOME IS WHERE THE ARMY SENDS YOU

If your soldier is Active Duty Army, chances are you will experience a Permanent Change of Station (PCS), a move to a new duty station, every three years or so. If your soldier is in the Reserve or National Guard, this won't apply to you as much, but you may experience a move if your soldier is promoted or changes his or her MOS (Military Occupational Specialty). Moving with the military can be confusing and stress-inducing, especially if you're moving away from an area you have grown to love or to an overseas location where you don't know anyone or speak the language. At the same time, it's very exciting—you get to explore a new state or country, meet new friends and gain new experiences. Not many people get this kind of opportunity…and have it paid for by their employer.

Some soldiers are allowed to create a "wish list" of the top four or five places they'd like to be stationed. If their MOS matches up with a need the Army has in a location on the wish list, you may get lucky. Otherwise, your soldier will receive orders for a new duty station, and you will have no say in the matter. But, a word of caution: since things change often in the military, don't make any plans until you actually have the PCS orders in hand.

There is a lot to know about moving to a new duty station (referred to as PCSing). After receiving orders, the best place to start is to visit the base relocation and housing office, followed by the transportation office. These offices should inform you about your three moving choices—do it yourself (DITY), commercial movers (TMO) or a combination of the two. A June 2011 survey done by *Military Spouse Magazine* rated the best ways to PCS according to their readership:

68% – TMO, government move
22% – DITY, moving truck
 6% – PODS, other moving service
 4% – Yard Sale, leave it behind

The housing and transportation offices will explain things such as packing, unpacking, household item weight allowances (dependent on your soldier's pay grade) and moving pets and cars. This is also where you'll find out about per diems, which differ for Active Duty vs. Reserve or Guard families; be sure to inquire about temporary lodging expenses (TLE) to cover lodging needs before you get settled into your new home. You may be on a waiting list, so visit your housing office right away to inquire about available housing at the new duty station. How long you're on a waiting list depends on various factors, such as rank, number of family members, genders and ages of children and housing availability.

A PCS can be an enjoyable experience, and a lot of families turn it into a paid-for family vacation. Since your soldier will normally get ten days off to accomplish the move, if you do your research ahead of time, you can turn the PCS experience into a grand family adventure. The best part? If you do it frugally, you may actually make money in the process with per diems and allowances.

You will also hear the term TDY (temporary duty station) often. This refers to short-term assignments in which your soldier will need to travel to a new geographic location. TDYs usually come with a per diem and will cover lodging and food expenses.

In military housing, a family is normally allowed to have two pets. There may even be a veterinary clinic on post.

There are several housing and relocation resources for families and soldiers; here are a few:

+ View an interactive map that shows all U.S. Army posts in the United States and abroad at http://www.goarmy.com/home/soldier-life/post-locations.html.

+ View government-subsidized base housing developments at https://www.housing.army.mil/ah. This site also has floor plans, airport information and driving directions, along with base in-processing and local community and city information.

+ Military OneSource has a Relocation Assistance Program to help ensure that your family makes smart financial decisions, plans a smooth move and receives all allowances and entitlements. They are available 24/7 by phone at 1-800-342-9647, or you can visit their website at www.militaryonesource.com.

+ CinCHouse.com, a name derived from the term "Commander in Chief of the Home," has a comprehensive list of relocation how-tos. There is also a discussion board so you can connect with women who live, or have lived, at your new duty station; they will give you the real scoop on what to expect. Visit www.cinchouse.com.

+ The MilitaryHOMEFRONT website has a section called HOMEFRONTConnections that enables you to meet and interact with fellow members of the military community, allowing you to share information and resources; visit www.militaryhomefront.dod.mil/.

ON VS. OFF POST HOUSING

Army life differs slightly depending on where you live. If you're involved in the military long enough, you'll probably experience many different Army installations and live both on and off post at one time or another.

Most of us already know what it feels like to live off base. You leave work, commute home and put the day behind you. You're able to decorate your house the way you want by painting, hanging photos and planting flowers. Friends or family can stop by to visit at any time, and you can park wherever you want in your driveway. Essentially, you have control over your home and life, without the base regulations. One notable drawback to living off base is that a soldier may have to wait in a long line to get on post for work, as all cars go through a security checkpoint.

If a soldier is married, he or she will be given the option to live off post and receive a BAH (Basic Allowance for Housing). If living on base, you will receive free housing in place of a BAH. Living on or off base is a personal preference based on what works best for you and your family. Some soldiers and their families need the separation of work and home life, yet others value the support and camaraderie of living on base.

There are pros and cons to each option; included are a few tidbits of information about living on base, straight from the mouths of seasoned military spouses:

+ Housing may be segregated based on rank, such as separate officer and enlisted neighborhoods.

+ Daycare is typically available on base, but there is often a waiting list. Sign up early if you know you're moving to a new post or will want to enroll your child in daycare in the near future.

+ You may share a driveway or backyard with your neighbors.

+ If you have an RV or trailer, it can be parked in the driveway for a maximum of 48 hours.

+ You must mow your lawn every week.

+ If the base has an unexpected gate closure for security reasons, you could be stuck inside, waiting to get out. An example of this situation could be if a child is reported missing.

+ You can't have friends pop over quickly to visit. In order to get a visitor's pass, a friend may need to get a background check, by having his or her driver's license run through the system, and a car inspection. This can take 15 minutes or up to an hour, depending on how many people are in line.

+ If something breaks in your home, you can call housing maintenance, and they will fix it for you.

+ It's nice to live close to the commissary because of the great deals to be found…just don't go on payday, because everybody else is there, too!

+ Utilities are government subsidized, so you can run your air conditioner as much as you want.

- Being on base during a deployment provides much-needed support from like-minded neighbors and friends who understand exactly what you're going through.

- You may feel more protected during a deployment.

 Wherever you choose to live, get involved with base activities or the FRG group. The camaraderie and support you gain will sustain you through a deployment.

FAMILY READINESS GROUPS: YOUR SUPPORT LIFELINE

If there is nothing else you take away from this book, I hope you learn one thing: the Army is a family. You are not alone, and there are many people to help you through any rough spots. Please get involved in your Family Readiness Group (FRG). Just as the Army talks with soldiers about the logistics they will experience during their service, the FRG communicates with spouses and significant others about what they can expect.

Fellow military spouses and your FRG leader are your best sources of support, especially during a deployment. They understand what you're going through better than anybody else, and your FRG leader can help you if the "deployment curse" rears its ugly head. Seek your FRG leader out before your soldier deploys, and make sure your phone number and email is in the group's family distribution contact list.

Kim, an amazing National Guard FRG leader, said, "Usually, I don't ever meet or hear from a spouse till there is a major issue in their family or home, and that is why FRG is here. We're not only here for the camaraderie and daily support, but for the really bad times when there is no one else you can turn to for help."

FRG leaders can help alleviate the stressors that a deployed service member isn't able to fix from afar. You should be able to call your FRG leader at any time of the day or night in case of an emergency. Utilize FRG services, and be sure to thank leaders for their help, as they are unpaid volunteers.

Of course, where a group of women gather, there may be gossip. Sometimes, women pull their husbands' ranks and talk down to wives of lower enlisted soldiers, or they simply gossip or complain. This may only be true in some instances, but it does exist. One of the best pieces of advice my husband gave me was, "Don't listen to what the other wives say about what is going on during a deployment or within our unit." This is because all soldiers have different missions on post and overseas, and what may be true for one is not true for all. A good rule of thumb is to not to get involved in gossipy situations.

If you live on post, check out the ACS (Army Community Service). This is a social services network providing a lending closet (you can even check out a coffee maker if you need to borrow one), volunteer opportunities and counseling for personal, family or employment issues.

DEPLOYMENT AND EMOTIONS

DEPLOYMENT:
THE EMOTIONAL MARATHON

In most cases, the inevitable will happen: a soldier will be deployed. The purpose of a soldier's military career is to prepare for his or her role in a combat situation; Active Duty soldiers train for a deployment every day, while Reserve and National Guard soldiers train well in advance of being shipped out. They've trained hour after hour to know what to expect on their missions and what each day will be like. Army significant others and spouses, however, are not trained for deployments at all. We often have no idea what to expect in the coming months of a deployment, especially if it's our first one.

As I mentioned in an earlier chapter, my soldier left just weeks after we were married for a one-year deployment to the Middle East. While this is not uncommon in military marriages, it was the first deployment for me, and it was trying. I had not prepared myself for how hard of a year it would be without him. I cried at anything military-related for nearly a year and finally realized I had to turn the radio and TV off when military topics came on. It was just too hard to deal with the range of emotions that crept up from out of nowhere.

In addition to my own feelings, I also had to deal with talking about the deployment with others. When strangers heard that my husband was deployed, they often wanted to delve into my personal life. I learned to become a "master subject changer"; you'll discover that people will want to talk about military issues, rant about the politics of war or discuss the latest combat tragedy they saw in the news. Most civilians don't understand the military culture, and they don't know that these issues may be stressful to deal with while a loved one is deployed. They don't realize that we are worried about the safety of our soldier every day!

What I learned during the year apart from my soldier, through my own experiences as well as through talking with others, is that each significant other, spouse or child of a soldier experiences different feelings during a deployment. Every person is in a different stage of life: different age, relationship status and situation. Some women are experiencing a pregnancy, some people are new parents and others have several children. It's these different life situations that cause each person to react to a similar situation—deployment—differently. I learned a valuable lesson during my first deployment: all the feelings I was experiencing—sadness, loneliness, guilt, irritability, fear and anger—are all completely normal!

Unless you share your thoughts and feelings with others, it is common to feel as if you're in it alone. Fellow Army spouses and significant others were my lifeline during deployment. You'll find that they speak the same language and understand your thoughts and emotions—sometimes even more so than your best friends or family.

During a deployment, you'll have a few landmark events, such as anticipation of leave or homecoming, which may affect your emotions. Remember: the emotions surrounding the abnormal event of a deployment are all normal. Included are some of the key stages of deployment, as well as the possible feelings you may experience surrounding these events.

Anticipation of Deployment

Before your soldier deploys, you may think about the year ahead without him or her, which will bring up a range of feelings. Sometimes you will be in denial that it is actually happening. You may be sad, angry, resentful or restless as the time approaches. In the few days before leaving, your soldier will mentally prepare for war and may distance from you emotionally. Likewise, you may feel like you can't put any effort into the relationship, since it is "going away" for an extended period of time, and you may distance yourself, too.

During Deployment

The Army traditionally has longer deployments than other branches, upwards of nine to 15 months at a time, with two to three months of training beforehand. Brutal, I know. This is where the long haul begins, and you must make the decision to get through it each and every day. When your soldier leaves, you may feel relief that he or she is finally gone and you can begin getting the deployment over with. Some people feel depressed, overwhelmed or without purpose. You may have trouble sleeping and experience anger because your soldier has left you, and you may also be disorganized when dealing with new duties and time schedules or feel just plain irritable about the situation.

You may also begin to encounter the "deployment curse." Anything that can go wrong will go wrong, and it often happens right after your soldier ships out! Inevitably, every spouse has moments during the deployment when life falls apart. Cars break down, sewer systems back up and sprinklers leak. Plan ahead to have a support network to manage these malfunctions *before* your soldier leaves.

Within a few months, you'll get into your groove. Some people value the newfound independence to do things they've had on their bucket lists. My friend Heather hiked the Grand Canyon while her boyfriend was deployed. She had always wanted to but never had time. Some women go back to school or take classes to keep busy. I started writing this book and took a part-time job! You will find yourself creating a new pattern as you accept the deployment and reorganize your life with your new responsibilities. If you are involved in your FRG (Family Readiness Group), you will be meeting new people and creating new support networks.

About halfway through deployment, give or take a few months, your soldier will get to take leave, or R&R, to come home to see you. Hooray! Leave occurs anywhere from one month after your soldier arrives in country or up to one month before returning home. Your soldier should receive two weeks off if he is on a deployment longer than six months. It is amazing to have your soldier home, and there is nothing better than seeing him or her after months of being apart. The anticipation of leave will have you excited for weeks!

But while it's great to have your soldier home, I'll fill you in on a little secret. You've been on your own for approximately 4-5 months or so, and you've finally hit your stride as the sole care provider. Your house, work and life seem relatively settled and manageable. If you have kids, they're finally used to their new routine. You're in a groove. Then, your soldier arrives for two weeks and all bets are off. Of course, you want him or her home; that goes without saying. But what people don't tell you is that it can be stressful. Some spouses and significant others have anxiety surrounding the leave. You and your soldier may have a massive case of nerves about seeing each other again, and you might have a feeling of resentment toward needing to drop everything you spend your time on to fit a year of time together into two short weeks. It's hard to balance work, friends, extended family and your quality alone time in fourteen days.

The best advice I received is to take it slow, don't be over-scheduled and keep the lines of communication open. Accept that your soldier may take a few days simply to catch up on sleep after traveling and will need to adjust to not being at work. He or she may also want to fit an entire year's worth of activity into two weeks and will be supercharged to see everyone and do everything.

 Don't plan a big trip over leave. Leave dates are subject to change at any time, and it could leave you with a non-refundable plane ticket you can't use.

During a monthly FRG meeting, about seven months into a deployment, the MFLC (Military Family Life Consultant) was talking through a "Stages of Deployment" presentation and asked how everyone was feeling. A wife spoke up and told the group she just felt numb. She didn't care about much of anything and found herself wanting to spend more and more time alone. The MFLC got excited and said, "Oh, you're in stage three! That is completely normal!" This Army spouse was relieved to know that what she was experiencing was normal, and it helped her accept her feelings and process through them.

Anticipation of Return

Towards the last month or so of the deployment, you will begin to fantasize about your soldier coming home. This is an emotional time, because you start to think about adjusting back to life the way it was before the deployment. You may want to look perfect or have the house in perfect shape when your loved one returns. You may rush to try to finish all the projects you wanted to accomplish throughout the deployment. You may be any combination of excited, nervous, restless, irritable or apprehensive. This is all okay and normal. The homecoming is a big deal and another big transition.

In my own experience, 11 months into deployment, my husband and I had some unpleasant phone calls. I was really stressed out heading into our eleventh month apart, as I was trying to finish my projects and deployment goals, as well as prepare for his return. He kept talking about all the things he wanted to do right when he got back, even things he didn't particularly enjoy before he left (golf, for example). Of course, I knew I wouldn't be able to stop everything I was working on to join him in all these activities. I would have liked to, but I knew it wasn't realistic with work and other commitments.

Knowing I couldn't join him stressed me out, because I wanted to spend time with him when he returned. A few phone calls later, he admitted he wouldn't do all of the activities he'd mentioned, but that just talking about them made him happy and feel closer to being home. This was common, as many men in his unit mentioned that their wives were at the peak of stress within the last month of the deployment. Again, this is a natural progression. It's normal to want to have accomplished everything you planned on doing while your service member was gone and to be nervous upon his or her return. Be sure to communicate openly and honestly about how you're feeling. Hopefully, after you both admit to being stressed, you can laugh about it later.

The Homecoming and After Deployment

The actual homecoming is a "hurry up and wait" situation. Usually, you'll hear what flight your soldier will be on 48 hours in advance. My sister-in-law, Tracy, an Air Force wife of 23 years, said that she didn't believe her husband was coming home until she saw the whites of his eyes at the airport. That about sums it up!

While the waiting and uncertainty is difficult, reintegration can be tough, too. It was best said during one of our Yellow Ribbon Reintegration Program events that soldiers will have a huge adjustment period upon returning home. They have been in deployment status for six to 12 months and simply don't know how to act around anyone but the soldiers in their unit. These are the people they talked to and decompressed with on a daily basis. They have had constant military structure, as deployed soldiers eat, work, sleep and PT at the same time every day, whereas those of us at home have had chaos. Leaving the structure and adjusting to a new, less regimented lifestyle is difficult for most soldiers, and this is a time when the personal attributes discussed earlier (positivity, optimism, flexibility, patience and resilience) come in handy.

In addition to adjusting to home life, your soldier might be exhausted from traveling. If he or she is coming from overseas, your soldier may need about 48 hours of off-and-on sleep to catch up. Don't plan any big parties; wait to see how he or she is adjusting, and take things slow. If you do attend social engagements, do them outside of your home; this way, when your soldier is done being social, you aren't stuck entertaining guests, and there will be an "escape route" from the party. Remember: it may be stressful for soldiers to reintegrate into an unstructured, fast-paced life—things as simple as grocery shopping may become over stimulating situations.

Reintegration can be tough for spouses and significant others, too. You may mourn the loss of your freedom and independence while adjusting back into previous roles and responsibilities. After about two weeks of settling in, you may need to recreate routines and discuss your expectations of marriage or your relationship. You may feel emotionally distant, even while you're physically together. It can take up to six to 12 weeks after the homecoming to feel "normal" as a couple again, and it can take even longer if your soldier is experiencing Post-traumatic Stress Disorder (PTSD).

Two additional scenarios which are very common among returning soldiers that you should keep an eye out for are:

- **Aggressive Driving** – Soldiers have likely driven without traffic laws while deployed, so they may have road rage and be more aggressive than normal when driving on our structured streets.

- **Excessive Spending** – Active Duty soldiers will make more money during a deployment, and that money starts to burn a hole in their pockets while they're away. Upon return, they may feel like they are entitled to large purchases, such as guns and big screen TVs.

Every couple experiences deployment a little bit differently, and it is so important to talk openly to one another about what you're experiencing; if it is hard to communicate, consider talking to a counselor. It is easy to assume your partner thinks a certain way, but you don't know until you communicate. Seasoned Army spouses talk about how some deployments are harder than others. Each deployment is different, but none are easy.

"Deployment is like running an emotional marathon that you can't train for!"
— Army saying

 If your service member is Reserve or National Guard, be sure to attend the Yellow Ribbon Reintegration Program event at the end of a deployment. You'll be briefed on insurance benefits (and how long they'll last upon his return), PTSD signs and symptoms and how to make reintegration a smoother process for your family. Daycare is usually provided and paid for during Yellow Ribbon events. Learn more about the Yellow Ribbon Reintegration Program at www.yellowribbon.mil.

RESOURCES

There are several excellent resources to help guide you through a deployment; a few are:

+ *Surviving Deployment: A Guide for Military Families,* by Karen M. Pavlicin, is a resource for helping turn a "challenging situation into a positive experience."

+ *Faith Deployed…Again; More Daily Encouragement for Military Wives,* by Jocelyn Green, offers encouragement for getting through tough military situations; visit www.facebook.com/faithdeployed for more information.

+ Information and resources for military families can be found at www.survivingdeployment.com.

+ Suzanne Phillips, Psy.D., ABPP, has done a lot of research on military families. She has a blog and Facebook page with helpful articles on topics such as anger management for couples, military trauma and resilience. Visit http://blogs.psychcentral.com/healing-together.

+ Military OneSource has a section on its website specifically for deployments. Visit www.militaryonesource.com and click the "Military Life & Deployment" tab.

15 TIPS FOR DEALING WITH A DEPLOYMENT

A deployment can be tough, but there are some ways to make it a little more bearable. Included are 15 tips for dealing with deployment:

1. **Stay busy.** Seriously. I hated reading this in every piece of literature on deployment I picked up, but it's true. I took a part-time job just so I didn't have as much time to think about my husband being away and how long it took him to email me back. The more you do, the more you will have to talk about too.

2. **Communicate regularly.** Set a time to communicate with your spouse on a regular basis—whatever works for the two of you and with your soldier's schedule. When you talk, be honest about how you're feeling. Try to be positive and upbeat, but do communicate in an open and honest way about how you feel as you progress through the stages of deployment.

3. **Seek help.** Have a support group of friends, family or fellow Army spouses and significant others. Don't try to "be strong" and do everything on your own. Join some of the many blogs and Facebook pages available for Army spouses; it is good to have the camaraderie of people going through the same thing you are.

4. **Transition household duties.** Take over household responsibilities before your soldier leaves so you know what to expect.

5. **Remember the "deployment curse."** Anything that can possibly go wrong will go wrong while your soldier is away. Have a support network in place prior to your soldier leaving so that you have somewhere to turn during these times.

6. **Set goals for your time apart.** What have you always wanted to do, or where have you wanted to go? Try to make it happen.

7. **Have fun.** Find enjoyable activities to keep yourself and your family occupied.

8. **Vary your form of communication.** Try letters, video conferencing (Skype, FaceTime, etc.), phone calls and emails; just find what works best for the two of you. Also, keep a list of topics to discuss so you remember what you wanted to talk to your soldier about when you get a call.

9. **Talk with someone.** Contact the MFLC (Military Family Life Consultants) and make an appointment to talk. If you don't feel comfortable visiting the psychologist on base, work through Army OneSource for free counseling sessions. The American Forces Press Service stated in 2010 that Army wives whose husbands deploy, seek mental health services at a

higher rate than others, and the longer the deployment, the greater the emotional impact.

10. **Remember it isn't permanent.** This too shall pass. The feelings you're experiencing during the deployment will not last forever.

11. **Know that no news is good news.** Seriously, no news is typically good news in deployment situations.

12. **Be selective about watching the news.** Absolutely DO NOT believe everything you see on the news. The media needs ratings, so they dramatize and sensationalize what you are watching. Their facts are not always correct, either.

13. **Be creative with care packages.** It helps to pick things up that you think your soldier will like when you're shopping. Collect these items for a few weeks, and then send them together in a care package. Find a card that expresses how you're feeling at the moment; even a card saying, "I love you and miss you," goes a long way in boosting your soldier's morale.

14. **Mail care packages properly.** Go to the USPS and pick up Priority Mail packages in different sizes, along with mailing labels and customs PS Form 2976-A. Ask a USPS employee to help you fill out the first one and keep a sample for future mailings. Priority mail is the most cost-effective and reliable way to mail packages overseas to an APO (Army Post Office) address.

15. **Attend a Strong Bonds seminar.** Before and after deployment, attend a Strong Bonds seminar together. Strong Bonds is a chaplain-led program for single soldiers, couples and families, which works to build relationship resiliency. Visit www.strongbonds.org.

Family emergencies are handled through the Red Cross, and it is the same process used for emergencies during Basic Training. If you can't access your soldier via phone, the Red Cross can; call them at (877) 272-7337. Have the following information ready: soldier's full name, rank, branch of service, social security number, date of birth, military address and, for deployed service members only, information about the deployed unit and home base unit.

METHODS OF COMMUNICATION

Imagine: only 30 years ago, letters were just about the only form of communication available during a deployment. Today, with modern technology, we have so many more options. The first time I saw my husband's smile on Skype after two months apart, I broke into tears, because I was so happy to actually see his face.

But while modern technology is great, you should know that there will be communication obstacles, because technology won't always work when you want it to. Experiment to find the best method of communication; if one isn't working, switch to another. Kelly, a military girlfriend facing her first deployment, said her boyfriend assumed that, because of technology, they weren't going to write letters. She set him straight by explaining why it was important for her to write letters…and she even sent him off with some preaddressed envelopes.

Included are a few communication options you can utilize during a deployment:

- **Letters** are still an amazing form of communication. Thoughts can be expressed in your own time and flow onto paper differently than they do on the phone. They only cost you the rate of a standard postage stamp since they mail through an APO (Army Post Office) address. Getting mail from my deployed soldier was my favorite way to communicate. I will cherish our deployment letters for a lifetime!

- **magicJack** is a device that allows you to make free phone calls throughout the U.S. and Canada, with low rates for international calls. Simply purchase a magicJack for $39.95 online, plug a home phone into it and then plug the device into the USB port on your computer. It will assign you a local phone number, and then you can start calling; it has free voicemail, too. As a spouse or significant other, you have no control during a deployment, so it is a small luxury to be able to call your soldier when you want to—even if you only get to leave a message.

- **Skype** is a service that provides free video conferencing and inexpensive mobile calling. My husband and I found this to be hit-or-miss technology—sometimes the Internet connection was too slow for video or the sound wouldn't work properly. When Skype works, though, it's wonderful to be able to see each other. Go to www.skype.com to set up a free account.

- **FaceTime**, from Apple®, is a free, web-based service that allows you to make video calls from certain Apple® products, and all you need is WiFi. The cool feature with FaceTime, when using an iPhone, is that it has two cameras; if you want to, you can show the person on the other end exactly what is happening around you. This way, your soldier can see what you see, rather than just see what is behind you.

- **SPAWAR Calling Card**, from SPAWAR Internet Café, is a calling card your soldier can buy through the company's website, www.spawarcafes.net. It comes in handy when traveling; all a soldier has to do is dial a phone number, area code first, and then enter his or her PIN.

However you decide to communicate, know that maintaining an emotional connection is essential for sustaining a relationship during a deployment.

> *"If two people can't see each other,*
> *then it's impossible to communicate."*
> — Unknown Roman warfare expert (63 AD)

Before a deployment, talk with your soldier about how he or she is picturing communication. Your loved one may not know what kind of phone access or Internet connections will be available until a few days after he or she gets in country, but discussing communication methods will help clarify your expectations.

OPERATIONS SECURITY (OPSEC)

I learned about Operations Security (OPSEC) the hard way. During my husband's deployment, I posted on Facebook that I was "Kuwaiting for a call." As I hit "Enter," I felt very clever and funny…but that feeling didn't last long. Within minutes, I was scolded by two well-seasoned military wives, both telling me that it is a "no-no" to talk about troop movements. The sooner you learn this, the better.

There is a lot of information your loved one cannot tell you about what he or she does daily—especially if he or she is deployed. A fellow Army wife mentioned that, when her husband was deployed to the Middle East, he worked in a high OPSEC position. For months, their conversations were one-sided, with just her talking! He couldn't share anything about his day, and it made for rough phone calls. If this happens to you, do not take it personally; you must accept and respect this without getting upset.

If you want to protect the safety and well-being of our troops, the following are the OPSEC rules you must know. These can be found online at

http://www.opsecprofessionals.org/articles/OPSEC_Rules.html.

Please share these rules with other Army spouses and significant others.

OPSEC Rules

1. Do not post exact deployment dates or redeployment dates.

2. Do not reveal camp locations, including nearby cities. After the deployment is officially announced by military officials, you may discuss locations that have been released, normally on the country level.

3. Do not discuss convoy routes (e.g., "We traveled through Takrit on our way to X.")

4. Do not reveal detailed information on the mission, capabilities or morale of a unit.

5. Do not reveal specific names or actual nicknames.

6. Do not discuss personnel transactions that occur in large numbers (e.g., pay information, powers of attorney, wills, etc.).

7. Do not reveal details concerning security procedures, response times or tactics.

8. Don't discuss equipment or lack thereof, including training equipment.

9. Don't speculate about future operations.

10. If posting pictures, don't post anything that could be misconstrued or used for propaganda purposes. A good rule of thumb is to look at your picture without your caption

or explanation and consider if it could be re-captioned to reflect poorly on coalition forces. For example, your image might show your soldier rescuing a child from a blast site, but it could be re-captioned to insinuate that the child was being captured or harmed. (It's happened!)

11. Avoid the use of online count-up or count-down tickers for the same reason as rule #1.

12. Be very careful if posting pictures of your loved one. Avoid images that show significant landmarks near his or her base of operations, and black out last names and unit affiliations.

13. Do not ever post information about casualties (coalition or enemy) before the official release of the information.

14. Do not pass on rumors. (e.g., "I heard they're coming home early," etc.)

In addition to OPSEC, there is also PERSC (personal security). Don't post pictures online showing names, ranks and other personal information. Don't let the public know that your husband is gone for an extended time period. Assume that your calls, Facebook page and emails can and will be intercepted. If someone asks you a question you can't answer, tell him or her that you don't know. Try to speak in terms of special dates that only your loved ones know. For example, if your wedding anniversary is on May 15th and he is coming home on leave May 20th, he can say, "I will be coming home five days after our anniversary."

Be smart. Don't update your status with this information, with your anniversary date listed for all to see in your Facebook profile. They didn't come up with the saying, "loose lips sink ships," for nothing!

Don't discuss the following in ANY form or fashion, even if you see others doing it first:

- *Troop movements*
- *Deployment dates*
- *Weaponry capabilities*
- *Unit capabilities*

PTSD SIGNS AND SYMPTOMS

Thankfully, the military is now recognizing PTSD (Post-traumatic Stress Disorder) as a serious issue and is helping service men and women deal with it after deployments. PTSD is a real and debilitating disease that affects many soldiers who've deployed to combat situations.

The National Center for PTSD defines it as "an anxiety disorder that can occur after you have been through a traumatic event. A traumatic event is something horrible and scary that you see or that happens to you. During this type of event, you think that your life or others' lives are in danger. You may feel afraid or feel that you have no control over what is happening." Soldiers bring this traumatic event home in the form of Post-traumatic Stress Disorder, and it can have serious consequences on their lives and the lives of those around them.

When most soldiers come home, there is a slight readjustment period as they transition back to normalcy within their homes and communities. While needing time for readjustment is normal, there are many symptoms for PTSD that you should watch for in your soldier. Keep in mind that some symptoms begin immediately after the traumatic event, but PTSD may also surface months or years down the road.

The most common symptoms are:

+ **Avoidance** – Avoiding people or events that bring up memories of the event. Sometimes this keeps soldiers from pursuing counseling that could help them, as it is too painful to bring the memories up to the surface.

- **Flashbacks** – Someone experiencing PTSD may have nightmares, or the event will play itself repeatedly in his or her mind, as if it were actually happening. These flashbacks can come back at any time and in any place.

- **Hyperarousal** – During combat, soldiers need to always be on alert for danger, and this is something they can bring home with them. They may be jittery and "on the lookout" at all times, even in day-to-day situations. This hyperarousal can cause side effects such as anger, irritability, trouble sleeping, startling easily and trouble focusing.

- **Numbness** – Soldiers may come back feeling numb and unable to express their feelings the same way they did before the war. When they don't have positive or loving feelings to express, sometimes they distance themselves from relationships they used to enjoy. They may also be disinterested in activities they used to enjoy or repress painful memories from the war.

Keep an eye out for these symptoms in your loved one. If they persist for more than four weeks after your soldier returns from a traumatic experience, or if they interfere with life, work or relationships, it is time to seek professional help. If your soldier increases his or her use of drugs or alcohol, becomes violent or feels shame, despair or hopelessness, find someone to talk to about the next steps toward getting your soldier some help. Ignoring these symptoms will only prolong your soldier's suffering.

Soldiers with PTSD need more than your love—they need professional help and care. If you don't know who to turn to for help, start with your post's chaplain. There should also be a combat stress counselor on post you can speak with, and VAs and Veterans Centers focus on treatment options as well. It will not hurt your soldier's career if he or she is treated for PTSD symptoms.

RESOURCES

There are many resources for dealing with PTSD; a few are:

+ Resources for veterans with PTSD can be found on the Military.com website, http://www.military.com/benefits/ resources/ptsd-overview.

+ *Healing Together: A Couple's Guide for Coping with Trauma and Post-traumatic Stress,* by Suzanne B. Phillips, Psy.D., ABPP, and Dianne Kane, DSW, contains a step-by-step program inspired by the authors' clinical experiences with first responders and their families, who suffered in the aftermath of 9/11.

+ *Once a Warrior—Always a Warrior,* by Charles Hoge, M.D., details how to make use of the very necessary warrior skills that soldiers bring home, instead of just seeing these skills as symptoms.

ARMY KIDS: RESOURCES FOR MILITARY CHILDREN

Whether it is during a deployment, Basic Training or military training separation, each child will have his or her own unique way of dealing with the situation. Some children may lash out in anger, while others may retreat and withdraw. One of the most important things you can do as a parent during this time is to stay healthy and take care of yourself first and foremost. Establishing stability and routine provides a healthy order to a household, and listening to and acknowledging a child's feelings is also important. As with other sectors of the military, there are several resources available for military families with children to help make things easier on the entire family.

One such resource is an organization called Flat Daddies (flatdaddies.com), which prints life-size photos of service men and women, also known as "flat daddies" or "flat mommies," which can help a child deal with separation. Family members like to take their flat parent with them to events during the year so their soldier is in pictures with friends and family; it helps families feel like their loved one isn't forgotten while he or she is gone.

Another great resource is Operation Give a Hug (ogah.org). These special dolls have a slot for a photo of the soldier on the doll's face and are often referred to by children as their daddy or mommy dolls. Kids carry them around, sleep with them and hug on them while their parents are deployed. Spouses and significant others love them too! After my husband deployed, I think our dog must have known that the doll was the only physical remnant of her soldier while he was gone; she kept stealing it off my bed, until I finally had to hide it from her.

Schools

If you are Active Duty living on post and need childcare for your family, look into the Child Development Center and Child, Youth and School Services (CYS) to discuss daycare options. You will need to register to enroll children in the programs, and just like with housing, chances are you may find yourself on a waiting list. The fees for childcare are frequently determined on a sliding scale, based on wages earned. There may also be convenient DoD schools on post, but if you want your child to attend a public school, that option is available as well. Your best bet is to visit the post's school liaison officer to discuss options available to your family.

While there are many great websites and organizations with information about raising military kids, included are ten excellent children's resources.

1. **Operation Military Kids (OMK)** – Connects military children and youth with local resources; www.operationmilitarykids.org.

2. **Military OneSource** – Provides assistance with parenting, stress and much more; www.militaryonesource.com.

3. **Army OneSource** – Contains a section for child, youth and school services; www.myArmyonesource.com.

4. **Our Military Kids** – Provides grants that enable military children to participate in sports, fine arts, camps and tutoring programs while a parent is deployed or recovering from injury; www.ourmilitarykids.org.

5. **Military Child Education Coalition** – Provides resources about peer-to-peer programs for students who have been relocated, checklist for transferring students and art and space camp opportunities; www.militarychild.org.

6. **Military Family Blogs** – This list contains the top 25 military family blogs as of July 2011; www.circleofmoms.com/article/top-25-military-family-blogs-00916.

7. **Blue Star Families** – Supports, connects and empowers military families; www.bluestarfam.org.

8. **Operation We Are Here** – Provides a list of books for toddlers and teenagers to help them understand the military lifestyle and deal with deployments; www.operationwearehere.com/children.html.

9. **Scholarships for Military Children Program** – Funds scholarships for military children through the purchase of products from participating companies selling their merchandise in the commissary; www.militaryscholar.org.

10. **MFLCs** – Professional family counselors who are trained to talk to your child. Check with your local MFLC (Military and Family Life Consultant) to make an appointment or find out what books and resources are available; https://www.mhngs.com/app/programsandservices/mflc_program.content.

FUN FACT:

Do you know where the term "military brat" comes from?

The term "military brat" is commonly used to describe a child of a full-time service member of the armed forces who spends his or her childhood or adolescence moving to new geographic locations every few years. As a consequence, a military brat never really has a hometown.

Although many people think the term originated in our country, it originally came from the British Army. When a member of the British Army was assigned abroad and could take his family, the soldier was listed as BRAT status, which stood for: British Regiment Attached Traveler. Eventually, it came to refer only to the children of the military member, as the wives of the British Army soldiers objected to it referring to them. The term has been adopted worldwide and is commonly heard in reference to U.S. children. [5]

---

[5] Dunn, Michael M. "Note from AFA President – April, the Month of the Military Child." http://www.afa.org/PresidentsCorner/Notes/Notes_4-14-11.pdf.

RESOURCE

April is the Month of the Military Child. Learn more about how to help the health and wellness of your military child at www.health.mil/themes/military_children.aspx.

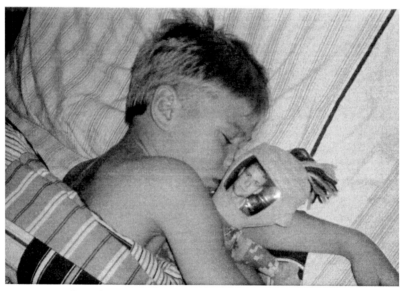

My friend Erica's son, Kolten, sleeping with his daddy doll.

THE GOOD STUFF

MILITARY DISCOUNTS AND HOW TO FIND THEM

As you're probably realizing by now, it can be difficult to learn the ropes of Army life, and it can be especially hard to find out about perks and discounts. The good news is, when you start looking for these discounts, you will find tons of resources for military families.

Many companies don't advertise that they have a military discount—you have to ask. Don't be afraid to do so!

Locally, start with your FRG (Family Readiness Group) leader or your Army spouse group. Make sure you are on their email distribution list for offers and events. They should have a list of local community businesses that support the military with discounts and special offers. Included are a few of my favorite "stumbled upon" resources; they offer amazing benefits for military families.

Discounts Listed by State: This website is great for many reasons, and one of them is the "Discount Map" tab, which shows military discounts by state. The site also has a live streaming of military family radio; www.guidetomilitarytravel.com.

Discounted Merchandise: The Military.com site has an organized listing of categories, such as apparel, automotive and electronics, which you can click through to see which companies offer discounts; www.military.com/discounts/category.

Free Photo: Canvas on Demand, a company that turns your photos into canvas portraits, will send a 16" x 20" canvas to any deployed soldier's spouse or mom; visit cool.canvasondemand.com to register for "Operation Hi Honey" or "Operation Hi Mom."

Free Photo Session: Operation: Love ReUnited is a nonprofit, fully volunteer organization that offers professional photography sessions to military families and members who are getting ready to deploy, are currently deployed or are coming home; www.oplove.org.

Free Photo Book: Friends and family can create a 20-page personal photo book and ship it to any APO, FPO or MPO address for free; uso.rocketlifeproduction.com.

Free Dog Tags: The Dog Tags for Kids Project is dedicated to helping soldiers in harm's way connect with their children at home. Specially engraved dog tags are provided free to service members for their children; www.dogtagsforkids.com.

Free Lawn and Snow Care: GreenCare for Troops is a nationwide outreach program coordinated by Project EverGreen, which connects local green industry professionals with families of deployed service members. Volunteers will mow your lawn or shovel your snow; www.projectevergreen.com/gcft.

Military Child Care: This site offers child care resources for military families, just click on the "Free Memberships for Military Families" link; www.sittercity.com.

Free Daddy Doll: Operation Give a Hug provides mommy and daddy dolls for children of deployed service members; www.ogah.org.

Free Hero Pack: Operation: Military Kits (OMK) partners with the community to produce Hero Packs, which are filled by nonmilitary youth and community organizations with mementos and items designed to help keep military kids connected with their deployed parents; www.operationmilitarykids.org/public/heropacks.aspx.

Free Banner: BuildASign.com provides free, customized welcome home banners for families of service members; www.buildasign.com/troops.

Free Books: Military OneSource has a section where you can order free books; www.militaryonesource.com/MOS/FindInformation/Category.aspx?NoCookieCTI=1&CategoryID=139.

Free Overstock.com Membership: Active, Retired or Reserve service members qualify for a free Overstock.com membership; send an email to militaryclubo@overstock.com using your .mil account with your name and proof of current or previous military service (e.g., rank, battalion, unit, station).

Guard and Reserve Commissary Discounts: The Guard and Reserve On-site Sales Program provides commissary benefits to Guard and Reserve members and their families who live in areas that are not close to an existing commissary store. You can save 30 percent or more; http://www.commissaries.com/guard_reserve_sales.cfm.

Free Theme Park Admission: Register for complimentary single-day admission to SeaWorld, Busch Gardens or Sesame Place; www.herosalute.com.

Free Care Package: Scion provides care packages for military personnel, including items like a beanie, deck of cards and complimentary hour of Internet access; www.scion.com/militarycarepackage.

Let's help one another! Post your favorite military resource or discount on the *Intro to Army Life* Facebook page: www.facebook.com/Intro-ToArmyLife.

You can get college tuition assistance as the spouse of a GI, and a soldier may also defer his or her GI Bill to a child to help pay for their college education. Read more about all the education benefits and tuition assistance programs available at www.armystudyguide.com/ education.

MWR: FREE FUN!

The MWR (Morale, Welfare and Recreation) philosophy is that Army soldiers need a balance of work and play in their lives to maintain their physical and mental health. The program offers services that reduce stress, as well as build skills and self-confidence in soldiers and their families. The MWR offers programs for vacations, sports and fitness, libraries, single service member programs, sports and recreation rentals, gym facilities and more!

The MWR offers several free and fun options that military families can take advantage of. Want to go camping? Check out a tent and fishing equipment. Are your kids bored? Enroll them in equestrian classes. The MWR even offers yoga classes and discounted tickets to sporting and cultural events in your community. Be sure to check out what MWR activities and programs are available at your current duty station, and then take advantage of them.

RESOURCE

Visit the Morale, Welfare and Recreation (MWR) website at www.armymwr.com.

THE GRATITUDE CAMPAIGN: HOW TO THANK A SERVICE MEMBER

The Gratitude Campaign™ was created after 9/11 as a quick, easy way for civilians to thank service members for their service. Founder Scott Truitt noticed that it can be awkward to approach strangers and thank them for their service, so he found a sign from the 18th century, which he adapted into the "civilian salute." The civilian salute is a specific sign that civilians can use to show their gratitude to those who serve when they encounter them in public, without even having to approach them— much like a military salute.

As military spouses and significant others, we know about the sacrifice involved in living a military lifestyle and what our soldiers give up to serve our country. They give up time with their friends and families, the lifestyle they're accustomed to living at home and, ultimately, they are willing to lay down their lives.

The Gratitude Campaign sign is intended to say, "Thank you from the bottom of my heart," for a soldier's service and sacrifice.

The organization's website explains, "To make the sign, simply place your hand on your heart as though you're saying the Pledge of Allegiance. Then, pull your hand down and out, bending at the elbow (not the wrist), stopping for a moment at about the belly button, with your hand flat, palm up, angled toward the person you're thanking." Next time you see a service member, show him or her your gratitude through this simple sign—they need the encouragement. To learn more, visit www.gratitudecampaign.org.

TOP 10 THINGS WE WISH NONMILITARY FAMILIES KNEW

Before becoming a military spouse, I would tear up when watching the video montages of service members reuniting with their families after a deployment. But honestly, I have to admit my understanding of, and involvement with, the military lifestyle didn't go much deeper than that. I didn't know anyone who had served in the military, nor had I experienced the military lifestyle growing up. Now, being neck deep in military life, I realize it's a *big deal*! Your life revolves around the military, and it can be tough, especially during deployments. If you love a soldier, there is no doubt that you're nodding your head as you read this— you *get it*!

According to the 2010 Military Family Lifestyle Survey conducted by Blue Star Families, 92 percent of military family respondents felt that the general public did not truly understand or appreciate the sacrifices made by service members and their families. Now, we aren't complaining about our military lifestyle. We have an enormous amount of pride for our soldiers and what they do, but civilian and military lifestyles are definitely different.

These are a few things I'd like nonmilitary families to know about Army lifestyle:

1. Your husband being gone for one to two weeks on a business trip is not comparable to my husband being deployed for three to 12 months in a combat zone. Unless your husband has been in a combat zone, and you have to worry about his life on a daily basis, you simply can't understand.

2. It is hard to manage on your own when your spouse isn't around. If your friend or family member is dealing with a deployment, he or she may act differently, as life stressors may drastically increase.

3. Acknowledging the struggles military families are going through, as well as being there as a source of support to listen and help, is extremely valued and appreciated.

4. Not many military spouses will ask for help, and they may be very reluctant to accept it. If you want to do something, don't ask if they need anything—just do it! Military parents rarely get time alone; offer to babysit, and let your friend or family member have some "me time."

5. Don't take it personally if a military spouse or significant other leaves your party early or ends a call with you when his or her spouse calls from Basic Training or overseas. Contact with our soldiers is so limited that we'll most often drop everything (a phone call, a social engagement, a favorite TV show) just to hear his or her voice and know they're alright.

6. We don't want to have a political debate over war just because our loved one serves in the military. We concentrate on the safety and well-being of our soldier, no matter what our political beliefs may be.

7. The smallest gestures sometimes mean the most. Just asking how our soldier is doing means a lot to us, and it helps to know that they haven't been forgotten while they're away. Someone once asked me, "What does your husband need, and where can I send it?" That was one of the nicest things I experienced while he was deployed.

8. Two weeks of leave seems like a long and short time to us during a deployment. It's long since we haven't seen our soldiers for anywhere from four to seven months, and it's short because we know they'll have to leave again soon so we have to cram one year into two weeks. It is hard to share our soldiers with everyone who wants to see them during the two weeks of the year they're home. Please understand if we can't fit everything in.

9. Coming home from a deployment is an extreme adjustment for our soldiers. Understand that your friend or family member may act differently for a while, until they reintegrate back into society. Also, help be on the lookout for PTSD symptoms, such as drinking or drug problems, shame, despair, anger and violence.

10. Some soldiers are career military men and women. They don't necessary "get out" automatically after a deployment—their lives and careers are focused on serving our country. Now, that is something to be proud of!

Share your "What I Wish They Knew" tips and stories on the *Intro to Army Life* Facebook page: www.facebook.com/IntroToArmyLife.

CONCLUSION:
WE'RE ALL IN THIS TOGETHER

This book is written as a tribute to the supportive and faithful military spouses and significant others across the globe. You carry a heavy burden when your service member is away, and while your soldier often gets thanked for his or her service, your service and sacrifice often goes unseen and unrecognized. Thank you for all you have done and will do in service to our soldiers and country by maintaining the home front. By doing so, your soldier is able to concentrate fully on his or her mission, without worrying that everything at home is alright. Here's to each of you who does so much and is an integral part of your soldier's success.

Spouses are referred to as "dependents" in the military, but we spend an awful lot of our time being independent as we manage homes, jobs, children, pets and many other factors in our daily lives. If you are new to Army life, the best thing you can do is educate yourself; my hope is that this book will give you enough resources and facts to enter the Army lifestyle a little more knowledgeable and inspired than when you started reading. It is by no means designed to be a comprehensive guide to the entire United States Army (or each subject discussed), but it should give you enough tools to enable you to feel confident and comfortable from the get-go, along with directing you to appropriate resources.

There are so many adventures to be had as a military family; with a good attitude and open communication, you will enjoy travel, new friends and new experiences. There will still be unwritten rules and etiquette you'll have to learn the hard way and moments when you'll feel like you can't go on...but trust me, you can!

Stay strong, be positive, keep the faith, ask for help, support your soldier and support one another. We're all in this together.

Never give up!

HOOAH!

ACKNOWLEDGEMENTS

Thank you to Rusty, my husband, for your unconditional love, support, patience and for introducing me to the military lifestyle. You continually amaze me and I love you more every day. You are my life and my rock.

Thank you to everyone at Aloha Publishing. Thank you, Maryanna Young, for your geniusness, amazing ideas, intuition, flexibility, friendship, inspiration and aloha. You encourage me always, and I thank you for believing in me. By doing so, you've helped many others who are entering the Army lifestyle.

Thank you, Kelly Antonczak, for your super feedback, ideas, encouragement and mad organizational skills throughout the process of writing this book. I know you understand what it is like to love a military man.

Thank you, Cari Campbell at Cari Campbell Design, for your creative skills and ability to totally read my mind to create the book cover I had envisioned.

Thanks to Dave Redford at Redford Design for creating my awesome website, www.IntroToArmyLife.com.

Thanks to Stacy Ennis for being the best copywriter/editor I've ever run across. Your attention to detail and finesse of the English language is fantastic!

Thank you, Nick Zelinger at NZ Graphics for your creativity, patience and talent in creating the book's interior design. You made the book come alive in print.

Thank you, Eleanor Jones, for the inspirational "Army Wife" coffee mug, which helped me battle writer's block and fuel my brain on Sunday mornings, as well as for your cheers of encouragement along the way. You've always been such a supportive auntie!

Thanks, Mom and Dad, for always supporting me, no matter what crazy project or endeavor I decide to undertake and no matter how stressed out it makes me. I love you both!

Thank you to everyone at Red Sky Public Relations. Jessica Flynn for sending me military-related articles and information and for the photo usage; Amanda Watson for buying me a facial just because my husband was coming home and she wanted me to feel pretty; Anna Gamel for letting me know about the FMLA; Heather Hill for sharing stories and sympathizing with me about the military lifestyle; Jenn Connor for the connections; and Danae Castellaw, Gloria Miller and Ashley Ford for the social media support!

Thank you to all the following people who shared their experiences and knowledge with me while I was writing this book: my sister-in-law, Tracy Mewes; Miranda Landaluce; Kimberly Callaghan; Katie and SFC Layne Drollinger; 1st Lt. Eric Price; SPC Travis Stanek; Sgt. Josh Stanek; and Patty Rowett.

Thanks to Suzanne B. Phillips, Psy.D., ABPP, who told me that a deployment is like an emotional marathon. Thank you for mailing me a complimentary copy of your book, *Healing Together: A Couple's Guide for Coping with Trauma and Post-traumatic Stress*. You've been a huge source of support to me!

Thank you to Timeless Photo for the uniform images, and thank you to Erica Lente for the photo usage of her son, Kolten.

Huge "HOOAH!" shout out to all the ladies in the Idaho Army National Guard Bravo Troop FRG group. Special thanks to Kim Callaghan for being a friend, confidant, shoulder to cry on and funny bone during my first deployment. You all helped me understand that I wasn't the only one going through a tough time and we're all in it together. Your support, advice and experience are undeniably what got me through some really hard days.

Thanks to Becky and Dale Wilson for having me over to dinner. Gestures of hospitality, like a home-cooked meal and fellowship, go a long way to help us through deployments.

A source of inspiration for my husband and me was found in Psalm 91, the Soldier's Psalm. Thanks to Steve and Monica Satake for bringing it to our attention and for being prayer warriors on our behalf.

Thank you to my friends and family, who supported and encouraged me throughout this process, too!

QUANTITY DISCOUNTS
ARE AVAILABLE

PLEASE EMAIL
ALLISON@INTROTOARMYLIFE.COM

Find us on Facebook at Intro to Army Life.